the book *of*
SPELLS

the book of
SPELLS

150 MAGICKAL WAYS TO ACHIEVE
YOUR HEART'S DESIRE

ELLA HARRISON

CONTENTS

CHAPTER 1 SPELLCRAFT

10 WHAT IS A SPELL?

12 WHO CAN PERFORM SPELLS?

14 WHEN TO PERFORM A SPELL

16 HOW SPELLS WORK

18 ETHICAL WITCHCRAFT

20 CREATING YOUR ALTAR

CHAPTER 2 THE SPELLS

26 BEFORE YOU BEGIN

Protection

29 ON-THE-GO PROTECTION

32 PROTECTION FOR YOUR HOME

38 BANISHING HARM

42 UNIVERSAL PROTECTION

Prosperity

47 ATTRACTING MONEY

54 PORTABLE PROSPERITY

108 DRAWING LOVE TO YOU

112 ENDINGS AND BREAK-UPS

Friendship and family

117 HARMONIOUS HOME

122 ANIMAL FAMILY

124 BEYOND THE VEIL

126 ENHANCED COMMUNICATION

132 MAKING FRIENDS

Joy and serenity

135 SUMMONING SERENITY

138 CULTIVATING CONTENTMENT

144 DREAMWORLD

148 MENTAL WELLBEING

152 SEASONAL CELEBRATIONS

Work and ambition

157 SUMMONING SUCCESS

164 RING IN THE CHANGES

170 SELF-IMPROVEMENT FOR SUCCESS

174 WRITE YOUR OWN SPELLS

178 CORRESPONDENCES

186 INDEX

190 SOURCES

191 ACKNOWLEDGMENTS

58 WISHING FOR ABUNDANCE

60 GOOD FORTUNE

Personal growth

65 SELF-REALIZATION AND EMPOWERMENT

68 INTUITION

70 SELF-LOVE AND BEAUTY

74 SELF-REFLECTION

78 DAILY GROWTH

Health and wellbeing

81 ILLNESS BANISHMENT

84 WELLNESS AND HEALING

96 EMOTIONAL HEALTH

Love and sex

99 ROMANCE

106 GLAMOUR

FOREWORD

I was raised in a (mostly) German family of people who practise and believe in magick - be that simple rituals such as tarot readings and communing with passed loved ones via pendulums, to being surrounded by crystals and having my palm read by my Oma. I was given *Teen Witch* by Silver Ravenwolf at the age of 11, which is where my dedicated practice of witchcraft started. Yet the biggest shift and growth in my path has been in the last several years - at the beginning of 2016, I started to truly become the witch I am today. My path has changed over the years, depending on which country we lived in, what influences were around me, and the availability of information at the time, and I am certain it will continue to shift and grow in the future. What always stayed constant was my admiration and deep love for magick and nature.

My goal with this book is to make the practice of magick accessible and approachable. Too often I have talked with people who are simply not sure how to get started, or are even intimidated by spells and rituals. I wanted to give you a brief introduction to what magick is, what spells are, how to protect yourself, and how to integrate magick into your daily life. In my opinion, life is full of magick, we just need to shift our mindset slightly to find it hidden in plain sight.

Spells and rituals do not need to be intimidating, and they should not be filled with ingredients that you need to spend a fortune on. For that reason, while I discuss some foundational components within this book, such as an altar and common tools, they are not obligatory. I want you to use this book to assist you in your own path. Take the parts you resonate with and leave the rest; change things up, make it your own. What works for me may not for you - for example, my personal path is very much influenced by traditional Wicca - something you may not chime with.

Your path may start with this book, which for me is one of the biggest honours, or perhaps you just want to add to your collection of books and this one looked interesting, which is also an honour! I encourage you to keep on searching for knowledge throughout your life. Wherever you are in your practice, may this book help you get started or assist you in moving forwards, or simply inspire you in your craft.

Ella Harrison

SPELLCRAFT

WHAT IS A SPELL?

When we intentionally direct energy to achieve a desired outcome, we cast a spell. You can draw this energy from the mind and will, ingredients or particular objects, or through practices and rituals.

Magic or magick

Different cultures have their preferred terms, practices, and concepts of what magick is. Some write it as "magic" instead of "magick", some call it "miracles", others call it "witchcraft", but magick is not one strictly defined concept – it's subject to individual interpretation. You could say our very existence, the perfect system of people, nature, and life itself is magick.

Your journey into spellcraft

The type of spell you cast will depend on your path, and there are many routes that can be investigated

– ceremonial magick, folk practices and traditional witchcraft, chaos magick. Whichever path or beliefs you follow, they are all valid. Spells can be simple or complex; they can consist of only one ingredient, or be part of a vast ritual, involving very specific tools and processes. Finding your preferred method comes with time and practice. Just as with cooking or baking, you may need to experiment to discover what works best for you.

As this is a lifelong journey, you have time and do not need to rush this process - in fact, you won't be able to. Depending on the outcome you desire, different types of spells will yield varied results - for example, spell jars usually contain or circulate their energies around the jar and work more slowly. Candles release energy quickly and efficiently. Knot magick draws in or releases energies, depending on whether you tie or untie the knots.

Adapting and personalizing your spells

Being resourceful is very important, but you cannot substitute all ingredients within a spell and hope for the same results. To return to the baking analogy, you can't make a carrot cake without carrots. However, spells can certainly be at their most powerful when they are adapted to suit your specific desires. You can use the spells in this book just as they are, or take them as your guide and personalize them if you'd prefer. It is your craft - make of it what you will!

WHO CAN PERFORM SPELLS?

Anyone can practise magick and witchcraft and perform spells. You do not have to be on any specific religious, cultural, or spiritual path to weave spellcraft into your life. Magick does not discriminate. If magick and spells fit into your existence, perfect!

Wicca and witchcraft

Not every witch is a Wiccan. Wicca is a religion that some people wish to be a part of or identify with. Witchcraft is simply a practice and is open to anyone, with specific ideas and application depending on culture, path, or religion. There are karmic concepts prevalent within witchcraft, such as "the rule of three" and "harm none", that have been popularized by Wicca, though not every Wiccan or witch lives by these. It's good to remain mindful of the problematic nature of pushing specific ideals from one religion onto another. You may choose for yourself.

Deities or gods

You do not have to believe in gods to perform spells, or work with deities if it feels unnatural to you. Atheist witches do exist – chaos magick, which relies on no specific belief and instead suggests that magical power comes from tested methods that have shown good results – makes a great example of just that. So while believing in your own work and spells is important, it doesn't mean you must now choose deities to work with if you cannot connect with that idea. For some, believing in gods or spirit beings is natural; for others, it simply isn't. Either way is valid, and your beliefs are your own choice.

Making spells accessible

Spells can be performed by anyone who wishes to do so, regardless of age, sex, gender, ethnicity, disability, or religion. Making magick accessible to everyone is essential. So if you find a spell in this book that requires tools or ingredients that you can't find, or steps or actions that you are not able to perform, adapt the spell to suit you and do not let it discourage or limit you. You'll find a list of correspondences that you can use as substitutes at the end of this book (see pages 178–185). Analyse the spells' symbolism and be inspired by them to create your own too (see pages 174–177).

WHEN TO PERFORM A SPELL

When should you perform spells? There really is no single correct answer. You can perform small rituals and spells daily, and cast lengthier spells dependent on phases of the moon or other cycles of nature, certain days of the week, or special celebrations in your life.

Know what you want

It's important for you to be aware of what you want to gain from the spell, and be willing to put in the effort required for the spell itself, as well as work outside of it. Remember that spells are both symbolic as well as effective in and of themselves. They can be useful tools for support and guidance, manifesting or celebrating goals, or simply as a way to live a more magickal life.

a spell will not go running for you, or make you lose weight overnight. Another example is the all-too-popular love spell. Be cautious with targeted spells directed at specific people, as sometimes we can cause ourselves more trouble than good, not knowing what a person is truly like, or not expecting any negative outcomes. As we are working not only with our own mind but also that of another, the equation is more complex. So if you are looking for some romantic love, calling that to you, rather than specifying "I want Bob to love me", might just do the trick.

Spell timing

What about certain astrological times? It simply depends on your own beliefs. If you are afraid to cast a spell during Mercury retrograde or an eclipse, for example, then do not conduct the spell, as your fear will seep in and possibly cause side effects, or the spell to fail. Although working through our fears can help, do not force or rush yourself if you know your experience will be negative.

Certain spells are most powerful or will yield the best results during particular phases of the moon or hours of the day, and many spells can be categorized and planned according to days of the week. You can check the correspondences on page 179 for which days and moon phases are traditionally considered the most potent time to perform your spell, but don't let that restrict you from exploring and conducting spells when it feels right. Spell timing can also be synchronized with your body's own cycles, to connect to your own inherent magick.

Intention is not everything

It is also important to remember that spells are not quick fixes and will not do all the work for you. For example, you may want to lose weight in a healthy and positive manner. A spell may assist in that, creating the right environment for you mentally, and possibly opening doors to fun experiences, but

HOW SPELLS WORK

Understanding how spells work is key to practising magick. Similarly to maths, you need the foundational "plus and minus" to be able to work on more complicated equations. If you are able to intrinsically understand spells, you can improvise with them, breaking them down or building them up on your own.

"Magic's just science that we don't understand yet." Arthur C. Clarke

Microcosm and macrocosm

The microcosm and macrocosm theory is the belief that our human body is a small-scale version of the universe, and, just as the universe has an influence over us, we have an influence over it, too. Particularly interesting is the idea that because humans have a mind, the universe too may have consciousness, or divinity. This creates a circle, meaning we too may be divine or connected to divinity. You could think of spells and magick as a drop in a still body of water – the drop creates ripples, spreading and creating an effect, showing everything is connected.

What to do if your spell isn't working

There are many reasons why a spell did not work. Perhaps it is still actively working and taking longer than expected – did you use the right ingredients to set up the timing of the spell? Using the element of fire – an element of fierceness and immediate effects – will tend to show results much faster than the element of earth, which is slow and steady (more on elements on page 182). Or perhaps you need to analyse your spell and consider if the ingredients were not quite right. Maybe you performed the spell in imperfect circumstances – for example, you rushed through it because you were tired. Sometimes a spell needs to be done periodically to show effectiveness, at other times you need to completely redo it, adding or changing a few things – that is why keeping a grimoire or spell book (see page 22) is important, so you can go back and analyse your work. It is also fundamental to fully commit to the energy of the spell, meaning your intention is important too – it is essentially one of the ingredients. Doubt can often interfere. If this is a concern, try to forget about your spell once you've cast it, so as not to interfere with its energy.

ETHICAL WITCH- CRAFT

The truth is, everyone will have a different opinion on the ethics of witchcraft. At the end of the day, you have to be comfortable with your craft, respectful of others, and mindful of your own actions.

Closed vs open practices

Almost every culture around the globe has its own beliefs and ritual-based practices. With social media, globalization, and increased travel, it is more important than ever to be respectful of other people's beliefs and practices. Closed practices are those into which one must be born, initiated, or formally invited to, and rituals and spells will usually be kept secret. Open practices are those that anyone can participate in. Knowing where your spells or practices come from can be tricky – often, they can be found in multiple countries and cultures, in both open and closed practices, so finding one definite origin can be difficult. Cross-referencing and simply looking up spells and practices online is recommended, or respectfully researching by any means you have available.

Ethical language

You may have heard the terms "black and white magick" – this terminology is to be avoided as it can be traced back to the racist beliefs that African/POC-originating practices are inherently evil. We must remember that in times gone by, magick was often used as a tool by oppressed people, who could not rely on help from other people or the law. Healing and hexing, blessing and baneful, positive and negative... there is a plethora of alternative terms that can be used instead.

The consequences of spellwork

One of the most important factors in witchcraft is understanding the consequences of your work. You should carefully think through all possible consequences of practising baneful or malicious magick, and be mindful of your actions. If you are comfortable with curses and hexes, there surely is a time and place for them, especially in cases of protection or justice-related matters, but when angry or hurt, we may want to curse immediately, without thinking rationally. Involving other people, and especially directing harm or forcing your emotions on others, can backfire if not very thoroughly thought through. A good rule of thumb is the age-old saying, "Do unto others as you would have them do unto you."

CREATING YOUR ALTAR

It is not obligatory to have an altar, but many practitioners like a space dedicated to their spellwork. Your altar is personal to you and you can set it up as you wish, but these items will be useful:

Candles

These come in all shapes, sizes, and colours. Depending on your spell or ritual, you may use taper candles, pillar candles, votive candles, or tea light candles. Each one will have a different burning time, making them more suitable for some spells than others. A list of colour correspondences can be found on page 178, though you can use a white candle as a substitute for any other colour.

Incense

You can use incense sticks in spells, or to cleanse your tools and ingredients (see page 27).

Runes

Runes, not to be confused with sigils, are the pre-Latin Germanic alphabet, used widely throughout Europe before Christianity. The most common version used in witchcraft is the Elder Futhark.

Runes have gained in popularity as a divinatory tool, and are also often used to inscribe and lend their meaning to a specific spell or working, and act in a similar way to sigils (see page 22). The common rune meanings are:

FEHU: Cattle, Elder, Wealth, Possessions, Luck, Divination and foresight

URUZ: Aurochs (Wild ox), Birch, Physical strength, Transformation

THURISAZ: Thorn, Hawthorn, Defence, Boundaries, New beginnings

ANSUZ: Mouth, Ash, Signals, Inspiration, Divine communication

RAIDO: Cartwheel, Oak, Circle of life, Travel and journey, Evolution, Perspective

KANO: Torch, Pine, Creation, Fire, Creativity, Transformation

GEBO: Gift, Elm, Partnerships, Exchanges, Contracts, Divine blessings

WUNJO: Joy, Ash, Harmony, Pleasure, Divine knowledge, Prosperity

HAGALAZ: Hail, Yew, Disruption, Uncontrolled nature, Protection, Power

NAUTHIZ: Necessity, Ash, Endurance, Survival, Transformation, Strength

ISA: Ice, Alder, Frustration, Introspection, Discipline

JERA: Harvest, Oak, Peace, Prosperity, Good crops

EIHWAZ: Defence, Yew, Release, Strength, Reliability, Protection

PERTHRO: Dice cup, Aspen, Mysteries, Initiation, Divination and foresight

ALGIZ: Elk, Yew, Protection, Divine connection, Ward off evil

SOWELO: Sun, Juniper, Success, Goals, Wholeness, Renewal

TIWAZ: Tyr, God, Honour, Justice, Warrior, Self-sacrifice

BERKANA: Goddess, Birch, Fertility and birth, Growth, New beginnings

EHWAZ: Horse, Ash, Transportation, Harmony, Teamwork, Loyalty and trust

MANNAZ: Humankind, Holly, The self, Memory, Social order

LAGUZ: Water, Willow, Healing and renewal, Dreams, Fantasies and subconscious

INGUZ: God, Apple, Male fertility, Gestation, Internal growth

DAGAZ: Day, Spruce, Breakthrough, Awakening, Self-realization

OTHILA: Property, Hawthorn, Protection in spiritual and physical journeys, Heritage, Abundance

Sigils

These are the broader symbols used in witchcraft, either instead of or in combination with runes. To create your own, try the sigil chart above. This can be adapted to include as many layers as you need to incorporate all the letters or characters in your language.

Pick a word or phrase you want to turn into a sigil. Now trace the letters in the chart to recreate your word or phrase in sigil format (see diagram below). Alternatively, a common system is to break down the letters into simple lines and curves and use these to then draw your own unique sigil.

Crystals

Crystals can be used as an ingredient in a spell, or worked with in isolation by harnessing their associated energies in various ways - either to spread energy within a room or space or for crystal healing. See pages 180-181 for a list of common crystal correspondences.

Knots

Knots are used to either tie in energy or to release it. They may be literal knots or even braids. Many practitioners keep cords for knots tucked away for later spells, once again using colour correspondences (see page 178) if desired.

Cauldron

The cauldron is used in spellwork as a vessel in which to combine ingredients and, burn them in order to release their energies. A cauldron can be a simple fireproof bowl or container.

Grimoire

Also called a Book of Shadows (BoS for short), or simply a spell book or journal, your grimoire will be your most important tool and the one and only piece of equipment that is absolutely necessary. In this journal, you will record your spells as well as any information significant to your craft. This could include moon phases, correspondences, personal practices or rituals, your dreams... Anything that may inform your spellwork can be included.

**THE SIGIL FOR
'MAGICK'** Keep it simple or
embellish and personalize it.

Tarot cards

These are divinatory tools and are used for either guidance or self-reflection. It's a good idea to select a tarot deck with clear imagery as your first deck (such as the Rider–Waite deck). Tarot reading is an excellent way to introduce magick to your daily routine by picking one card each day.

Carving tools

A variety of carving tools will come in handy throughout your practice. A boline is a more traditional tool for cutting herbs and carving candles or runes, but you can use thorns, needles, or even a toothpick just as effectively to carve.

Athame

A tool used mainly in ceremonial paths, such as Wicca and Thelema, the athame is a double-edged knife that is used in a ritualistic context. Its purpose isn't usually cutting, but rather to direct energy, mostly in casting a circle. In certain paths it is used in combination with the chalice to represent the union of The Lord and Lady.

Chalice

The chalice is a cup often used in ceremonies and rituals in combination with the athame. It is also the cup out of which a coven (a group of practitioners) or a solitary practitioner would drink during a ritual to connect with one another, or to the energies of the universe.

Containers

You will quickly learn that a witch can never have too many jars and bottles. These can be used either in spells themselves (spell jars, for example) or to collect herbs, crystals, and other ingredients.

Mortar and pestle

These handy tools are used for grinding ingredients and making powders.

Wand

Your wand is an extension of your arm, or so many practitioners say. Some traditions use a staff instead – both are used to direct energy. Your wand may be used to cast circles (see page 26) and to draw sigils or runes in the air.

Besom

A besom is a sacred broom to sweep away dust as well as negative energies.

Pentagram

The pentagram represents the five elements and the circle of life that connects us all: Earth, Air, Fire, Water, and Spirit. You can keep representative trinkets on your altar or the painted symbols. Alternatively, you could have a physical pentagram, in the form of a necklace or a planchette, for example. When you form the shape of a pentagram in your spellwork, it can be either to invoke or banish, depending on the direction in which you draw (see below).

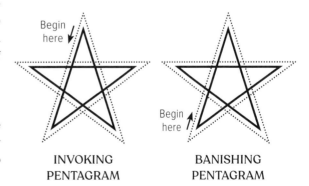

Begin here

Begin here

INVOKING PENTAGRAM

BANISHING PENTAGRAM

THE SPELLS

BEFORE YOU BEGIN

In magick, it is important to first ground and centre yourself and consider your protection – working with energy attracts energy to you, both from spirits as well as other practitioners or outside influences.

Casting a circle

Casting a circle is a popular way of saying "creating a protective space to work in." If you feel uncomfortable with the idea of casting a circle, you can always choose not to do so. This is a simplified version that you can use to cast and open the circle.

Stand in front of your altar or the space you wish to cast your circle, facing east. Hold out your index finger (or wand or athame) and walk clockwise, visualizing an energetic field or bubble forming around you. Walk the circle or turn around three times, with your finger tracing the circle. Say the words: "I cast a circle of protection, to work free from outside influence. So mote it be." To open the circle, face east, but now walk anticlockwise and say the words: "I open the circle of protection, blessed be" while visualizing the energetic circle lifting and fading away.

Grounding and centring

Usually done before and/or after spells and rituals, grounding and centring is an essential technique to remove stagnant energy, call your energy back in, or absorb extra energy from around you. Sit or stand and close your eyes, calming your body and mind. Focus on the energy within and around you. Imagine roots growing from your feet into the ground, where stagnant energies can flow out and be neutralized by the soil. Visualize energy returning back to you, so that your core is golden and glowing.

Cleansing

Think of cleansing as taking a spiritual shower – you remove any stagnant, old, and negative energies surrounding you and your space. There are many different cleansing techniques that you can use, depending on your preference and circumstances.

Smoke cleansing: Using smoke, such as through burning incense or herb bundles, to cleanse a space, tools, or ingredients is one of the more common techniques. You can make your own herb or floral bundles to cleanse, or buy incense sticks. Walk around your space, or move the bundle around items, to spread the smoke to purify the energies.

Sound cleansing: Using sound, such as a bell, singing, or even banging on pots, can cleanse and purify the surrounding area. You may prefer to use clear ringing sounds, such as bells, or you may prefer loud noises such as drums or pots. Simply playing music is not quite enough.

Energy cleansing: This technique requires no tools, but does require practice. Start by rubbing your hands together until they are tingly and warm, and slowly pull your hands apart, visualizing an energy flowing between them. You may with time and practice be able to feel the energy and a resistance when pushing your hands together again lightly. Then move your hands over tools, ingredients, or areas and visualize the stagnant energies evaporating. This is also a good technique whenever you need to raise your energies in spellwork.

Crystal cleansing: Certain crystals are associated with cleansing and protection (see pages 180-181 for correspondences). You can move these over your body, space, or tools and ingredients to cleanse them.

Physical cleaning: Physically tidying and cleaning your space, and washing your body, is another form of cleansing. Negative and stagnant energies will cling to dirt and messy areas. You can combine physical cleaning with spiritual cleansing by using cleansing sprays or floor washes.

Moonlight: The easiest form of cleansing is using the light of the Full Moon. This technique works best for your own body, as well as for tools that you can lay out on your windowsill. You can sit in meditation in the light of the Full Moon to cleanse, as well as recharge on Full Moon energy, which is both purifying and restorative.

PROTECTION

Protection magick is often considered the starting point,
as well as foundational knowledge, for any practitioner.
From maintaining an active home protection to shielding
from or even deflecting more targeted attacks, it is
thought to be generally good practice to always
have some sort of protection spell active.

29 ON-THE-GO PROTECTION

32 PROTECTION FOR YOUR HOME

38 BANISHING HARM

42 UNIVERSAL PROTECTION

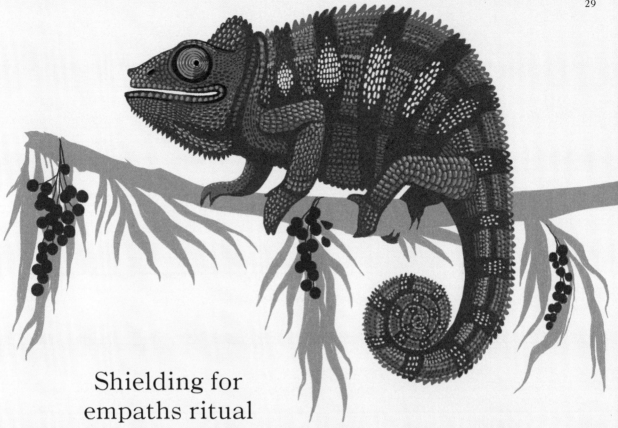

Shielding for empaths ritual

This technique is excellent for situations where you'd like to shield yourself from energies and emotions around you, whether it be in public, at a family gathering, in school, or at work. You can use this on the go without anyone noticing.

Centre and ground yourself, and start to imagine an energetic light forming in your chest. This light grows until it surrounds you completely. Imagine that light hardening, becoming an impenetrable diamond shield – you can still look through it and see what is going on around you, but anyone looking at you will see rainbow colours bouncing off your shield. Visualize your diamond shield having chameleon-like qualities, allowing you to blend in with your surroundings without anybody noticing you. Anyone who tries to project their energies onto you, consciously or unconsciously, will not be able to do so, as your shield deflects their energies back to them. You may also speak the words:

Shield me from view, protect me from you, may no energies pass through. So mote it be.

This shield will need to be fed energy to stay active, simply by you visualizing it being strong and impenetrable. However, it is not advisable to keep this shield on all the time, as you may become disconnected from your surroundings and other people. It can also be draining to maintain, especially at first. It is similar to working a muscle, so will become easier with practice.

BEST TIME Whenever necessary

Protection oil

TOOLS Dropper bottle or mason jar | Funnel **INGREDIENTS** 2 tbsp base oil (almond or grapeseed) | 7 drops sandalwood oil | 3 drops jasmine oil | 5–10 dried cloves | Pinch of dried witch hazel | Pinch of dried lavender.

This is an excellent spell oil to use daily or whenever you feel the need for extra protection. It can be used by itself or as part of other spells or rituals, and is perfect for dressing your protection candles. This oil will keep you safe from psychic or magickal attacks.

Start by cleansing your ingredients (see page 27). Add each ingredient to the bottle, while saying:

As the ingredients of this oil combine, may I be protected by the divine, so mote it be.

Shake the bottle to activate the ingredients' energies and pour one drop onto your skin, or any surface you wish to protect. Draw a banishing pentagram or your own protective sigil (see pages 22-23) with the oil and say:

May I be protected from all harm, so mote it be.

___

BEST TIME Anytime
NOTE For topical use only

Travel protection pouch

TOOLS Pen | Paper | Pouch or small bag **INGREDIENTS** A personal taglock (see tip) | Obsidian (or alternative protective crystal, see page 179) | 1 tsp camomile | 1 tsp black salt (see page 32)

Perfect for protecting yourself during day-to-day travel or long-distance journeying, this pouch can be tucked into your bag, car, or luggage.

Draw the protective rune Algiz (see page 21) or your protection sigil (see page 22) on your paper and fold it away from you three times, rotating it anticlockwise to banish. Then add your taglock, Obsidian, camomile, and black

salt to the pouch. Tie it shut and speak the words:

Wherever I travel, I am protected and blessed, so mote it be.

___

BEST TIME Before you travel
TIP A taglock is an object that connects your spell to a subject, such as a lock of hair, a picture, or a name written on paper.

Talisman enchantment

TOOLS Jewellery (a piece you wear daily, new or old)

Talismans or amulets have long been used around the world to drive away bad luck or bring in good fortune. In this spell, you create a protective talisman, requiring only yourself and a piece of jewellery.

Sit with a straight back and crossed legs, or in a seated position that's comfortable for you. Close your eyes or focus on your hands and take several deep breaths until you feel calm. Rub your hands together until they are warm and tingly. Now take your jewellery into your hands and visualize the energy from your hands flowing into your new talisman. Next, envision a bright light flowing from the universe above you and Mother Earth below you into your body, creating an energy circuit – flowing through you into the jewellery. Speak the words:

I bless and cleanse this [type of jewellery]. May it protect me from maleficent forces. From this day on may this be a sacred talisman tied to me alone. So mote it be.

BEST TIME Full Moon, Monday

Black salt

TOOLS Mortar and pestle **INGREDIENTS** Table salt | Dried eggshells (remove the white membrane layer) | Ashes (collected from incense or past spells) and/or charcoal | 1 tsp rosemary | 1 tsp black pepper

Salt is considered protective as it disperses negative energy. You can create your own black salt for extra protective and banishing properties to sprinkle on doorways and windowsills, draw sigils, or use in spells such as this.

Grind together the salt, eggshells, ashes and/or charcoal, rosemary, and black pepper, grinding anticlockwise, to banish. At this point you could also add in any other herbs associated with protection, for example, garden sage or lavender (see pages 182–185 for correspondences). Once finely ground, store your salt in a jar or bottle. Sprinkle this salt around your house and sweep it away every New Moon to renew it. Sweep from east to west, like the journey of the sun. When using, speak with intent of what you wish to achieve - let the words come to you intuitively, or say:

I cleanse this space and banish all evil and harm sent my way, so mote it be.

BEST TIME New Moon

Energy cleansing spray

TOOLS Spray bottle (preferably glass) **INGREDIENTS** Full Moon water (see tip) | A few drops lemon juice | 5 drops rosemary oil | 5 drops sage oil

This quick but effective cleansing spray is great for removing negative energies from a space, while also being very inconspicuous, making it perfect for broom-closet witches.

Add the Full Moon water, lemon juice, rosemary, and sage oil to your spray bottle. Shake well. Shaking it will activate the energy as well as mixing everything as much as possible (oil and water will never fully mix, which is fine).

Shake each time before using and spray with intent. You can frequently spray areas such as your bed, your room, or even your own energy field. When spraying, visualize a negative mist being cleansed away by your spray. You can also say the words:

The energy is cleansed and cleared,
blessed be.

BEST TIME Full Moon
TIP To make Full Moon water, fill a glass or jar with clean water and let it sit under full moonlight overnight (seal the glass if placing it outside).

Sleep protection pouch

TOOLS Small pouch or bag (preferably purple) **INGREDIENTS** 1 Amethyst crystal (or substitute, see page 179) | 1 tsp dried lavender | 3 pieces of dried lemon peel | 1 tsp dried camomile

Some people believe that when we sleep, we travel to the astral plane and are in a state of higher consciousness, which requires protection. Others simply wish to have a good night's sleep without nightmares. Place this pouch near your bed or under your pillow.

Cleanse your crystal (see page 27) and add it to the bag along with the lavender, lemon peels, and camomile. Sit with your bag in meditation and visualize a soothing purple light filling it. Speak the words:

May my sleep be protected from harm and
ill-will, so mote it be.

BEST TIME New Moon and Waning Moon

Hag stone blessing

TOOLS Cord or piece of string, arm's length | Hag stone

Hag stones – rocks with naturally formed holes found near beaches or rivers – have long been used in Celtic folk practices to protect from evil.

Sit in meditation with your stone, and visualize the stone and yourself forming a golden-silvery bond. Speak the words:

Hag stone of protection and magick, become my shield and guardian. So mote it be.

Take the cord or string, loop it through the Hag stone hole, and tie a knot at each end. Now either wear it as a necklace, or hang it near your front door. If wearing your stone, visualize it enveloping you in a golden silvery sheen of protection. If the stone ever breaks, it has used its power to protect you.

BEST TIME New Moon and Waning Moon

Protection plant spell

TOOLS Paper | Scissors | Black waterproof marker | 1 pot plant for each room in your house **OPTIONAL TOOLS** Quartz crystal tumbles (one for each plant)

Plants are excellent wards for your home, and can often indicate if you are under spiritual attack, as they act as first-line protectors.

Cut your paper into as many pieces as you have plants. With your marker, draw your own protective sigil (see page 22) or the rune Algiz (see page 21) onto each piece of paper. Bury the paper in each pot and say to each of your plants:

Spirit of this plant, I ask you to be my line of defence, be my protective ally. Blessed be.

You can now give the crystal to the plant by placing it next to it or in the soil.

Watering your plants and taking good care of them is very important. Use Full Moon water (see tip page 34) once a week as an offering. If you notice any well-cared-for plants suddenly withering, it means it has protected you, and you may need to put up more protective wards.

BEST TIME Waning Moon

A protected home ritual

TOOLS Besom or broom | Spray bottle | Incense | White candle | Lighter or matches **INGREDIENTS**
Black salt (see page 32) | Protection oil (see page 30) | Full Moon water (see tip page 34)

This home-protection ritual should be carried out once a month, ideally on the New or Full Moon. It is essentially a process of cleaning the house of dirt, cleansing the house of stagnant energies, and blessing the home.

Start by tidying your entire space – this step is very important, as negative energies cling to dirt and physical mess. Then, with your broom, start sweeping away the dust, making sure to sweep from east to west, like the daily journey of the sun. Now take your Full Moon water and pour some of it into your spray bottle. Move around your space, spraying each room three times.

Sprinkle a thin line of black salt at your front door. This will need to be swept away each month and relaid to keep up the protection. Dispose of the salt in the bin, as salt will ruin soil.

Next, take your protection oil and add a drop to your finger. With your oily finger, draw a protective sigil (see page 22) or the rune Algiz (see page 21) on each windowsill and door frame.

Light your incense, open all the windows, and move around the space one last time, letting the smoke disperse any lingering energies, which will exit through the windows.

Finally, light a white candle by your front door. This will be your protective candle, and you may light it whenever you are in the room.

———————

BEST TIME Every month on the New or Full Moon

Witch bottle spell

TOOLS Bottle or jar | 9 nails and/or razor blades, preferably rusty (only if using urine) | 9 pieces of broken glass or mirror | 9 thorns | Black candle (or black hot glue) | Lighter or matches
INGREDIENTS Black salt (see page 32) | A personal taglock (see tip page 30) | Vinegar or urine

Witch bottles have long been used as wards against evil – they act as a decoy, absorbing a curse or hex sent your way. It is advisable not to move the bottle once created, so be sure to bury it where it won't be disturbed.

Start by cleansing your space and yourself and casting a circle (see pages 26-27). Add the nails or razors (if using), broken glass and thorns, the black salt, and your personal taglock to the jar. Next, fill with vinegar or your own urine while keeping your intentions in mind.

Seal the jar and light the black candle, dripping the wax over the lid or cork so it may not be opened again. Speak the words:

May this jar protect me and my property, may any ill and maleficent intent be caught in it and drown. May hateful energies be caught by the sharp nails and glass, may the salt neutralize and render them useless. So mote it be.

Then you can open the circle. Now dig a deep hole somewhere in your garden or in a pot of soil and bury your jar. Know you are well protected.

BEST TIME New Moon and Waning Moon

Return to sender

TOOLS Cauldron or fireproof plate | Black candle | Lighter or matches | Boline or knife
INGREDIENTS 1 handful soil | 1 tsp sage | 1 tsp black salt (see page 32) | 1 tsp chilli powder | ½ handful dried lemon

This spell is intended to reflect a curse or hex back to the sender. You are not creating and sending out any curses, you are simply shielding and returning anything harmful that may have been sent your way.

Start by cleansing your space and yourself, and casting a circle (see pages 26-27). Add the soil, sage, black salt, chilli powder, and dried lemon to your cauldron, mixing them all together. Now focus on the spell sent your way, trying to energetically envision it, seeing its shape and colours in your mind, as well as the person who sent it. Once you have a clear picture in your mind, place your candle in the centre of the cauldron and light it. This candle represents the spell sent your way. Next, snuff out the flame in the soil mixture and, with your boline or blade, cut the top of the candle off to create a new bottom. Flip the candle upside down, and carve the new top into the typical pencil-like tip, exposing the wick.

Place the candle in the centre again and light it. As you do so, speak the words:

I return what you sent to me, may it never return, may the sender of this ill-will receive what they intended for me, so mote it be.

Continue to focus on the intent of returning the spell to the original sender and wait until the candle has burned down completely. Then you can open the circle.

You can now collect all the remaining ingredients and wax, dispose of them in a rubbish bin, and immediately remove them from your home.

BEST TIME Waning Moon

Hex-removing bath

INGREDIENTS 120ml (4fl oz) Full Moon water (see tip page 34) | 145g (5¼oz) Epsom salt | 1 pinch of cayenne pepper | 1 pinch of cinnamon | 1 sliced lemon

Bathing and water are considered both physically and spiritually cleansing, with many religions and cultures using water for sacred purposes. To remove a hex or curse from you, take this bath. It is not the right time to wash your hair or exfoliate your body – this sunrise bath should be purely spiritual in nature.

Draw your water and add your ingredients to the bath one by one, with intention. If you wish, you can speak out loud the purpose of each ingredient (see correspondences on pages 182–185). Sink into your bath and take several deep breaths. Focus only on your breathing for at least 10 minutes. Don't worry if your mind wanders, simply refocus on your breath. As you meditate, let the ingredients cleanse you from any curse or hex placed upon you. With the rising of the sun, you are cleansed and purified again. Once you feel ready to get out of the water, speak your own words or simply say:

The curse is broken, your power over me washed away, so mote it be.

Drain your bath and collect the ingredients. You can bury them somewhere far from your home or throw them in a bin.

BEST TIME As soon as you have identified or suspect being the victim of a hex or curse
Sunrise

All-round protection

TOOLS White or black candle (short burn time, birthday, or tea light candle is best) | Lighter or matches | Carving tool | Fireproof dish or bowl | Taglock (see tip page 30)
INGREDIENTS 3 drops protection oil (see page 30) | 3 dried rowan berries | 1 tsp dried camomile | 1 tsp dried lavender | 1 dried star anise | 1 tsp ground eggshells

This spell is intended to protect you from negative energies and entities. It can be adapted to protect a consenting family member or friend, or a pet.

Cleanse the space and light your altar candles. Cast a circle of protection, ground and centre yourself (see page 27), and invite the four elements and any deities, ancestors, or spirits you wish to work with into your circle. Meditate for at least five minutes to prepare yourself for this spell.

Take your candle and carve the rune Algiz (see page 21), or your own protective sigil (see page 22) into it. Pour a few drops of your protective oil onto your hands, and dress the candle from the centre outwards with the oil. Roll your candle in the dried herbs – use only one-third of the herbs, as you will use the rest later. Secure your candle to the fireproof dish. Sprinkle some herbs as well as the ground eggshells around it. Next, light your candle and bring to mind your intent: to protect. You could also visualize a glowing protective orb around you or your subject. Lightly hold your taglock above the flame, without burning it. Speak the incantation:

May I/subject be protected from all harm,
Disband all negative energy that may come
my/subject's way,
While this candle burns I do disarm,
And may positive energy be underway.
So mote it be.

Then burn your taglock in the flame. Meditate and visualize by your candle until it has burned down completely.

BEST TIME Every month on the Full or New Moon
WISDOM Moths have many spiritual associations
– some people believe they symbolize passed
loved ones or ancestors coming to visit.

BANISHING HARM

Protection jar

TOOLS Small glass jar | Small funnel | Pen or pencil | Black or white chime candle (or a hot glue gun) | Lighter or matches **INGREDIENTS** ½ tsp salt (Himalayan or black – see page 32) | ½ tsp dried rosemary | ½ tsp black pepper | Chips of crystals associated with protection (see page 179) | 1 dried bay leaf

This spell will provide you with constant protection in a jar, which can be placed under your bed or in another safe spot that you spend a lot of time in. If you notice the ingredients or colour going strange, or the bottle even cracking after time, the spell has worked and it is time to renew your jar.

Start by cleansing your glass jar (see page 27). Layer in the salt, rosemary, pepper, and the crystal chips. Draw either a protective rune on your bay leaf (see page 21), your own sigil of protection (see page 22), or the word "protection", and add it to the jar. Close the jar and seal it by dripping candle wax around the lid, or alternatively use a hot glue gun. You can speak a simple affirmation into the jar:

*May I be protected from
ill wishes and harm,
so mote it be.*

Shake every so often to activate the energies of the spell jar, and whenever you feel like you need a protection boost.

———————

BEST TIME Saturday, Waning Moon or New Moon

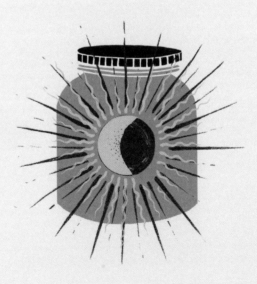

Spirit offering ritual

TOOLS Incense | Lighter or matches | Plate
INGREDIENTS Offering of food and drink

Building relationships with spirit allies will help to keep you protected. This ritual is both to pacify spirits you may have offended by living on land that is sacred to them, or by any other conscious or unconscious acts, as well as to create allies and spirit "friends" that can assist in your future practice.

Start by cleansing your space and yourself, and casting a circle (see pages 26–27). Sit by your altar and arrange the offerings. Hold your hands over them and visualize a light being emitted by your hands, washing over the offerings and cleansing them. Say the words:

May these offerings be cleansed and blessed.

Now invite the spirits – specific deities or ancestors, or simply the spirits that are all around you – by saying:

Spirits come in peace, enjoy this offering that I bring.

Light the incense and sit with the spirits, either in meditation or even talking, or eating something yourself. Once done, say:

Thank you for your presence, now may we part, return to your homes until we may meet again, so mote it be.

Open the circle and remove the offerings.

BEST TIME Daily or once a week

Full Moon ritual

TOOLS White candle | Lighter or matches | Needle, thorn, or toothpick | Cauldron or fireproof plate | Paper | Pen

The Full Moon is an excellent time for protection spells and rituals. You do not need to be able to see it for the energies of a Full Moon to still be in the air - though direct visibility certainly holds its own magick.

Start by cleansing your space and yourself, and casting a circle (see pages 26-27). Sit in meditation for at least 10 minutes, breathing deeply and absorbing the energies of the Full Moon by grounding and centring (see page 27).

Take your white candle and needle, thorn, or toothpick and inscribe the word "protection" as well as your own protective sigil (see page 22) or the rune Algiz (see page 21) into the wax. Light your candle and place it in your cauldron. Now on your paper, take your time to write down everything you wish to release. Fold the paper away from you three times, rotating it anticlockwise to banish, then burn it. Focus on the flame burning the paper, and the smoke rising from it. Then open your circle and eat to replenish your energy.

BEST TIME Full Moon

PROSPERITY

Prosperity spells, in all their forms, have always played a big part in witchcraft, as seen in folk magick, for example. They can be anything from charming a lucky talisman to more complex rituals intended to draw prosperity to you.

47 ATTRACTING MONEY

54 PORTABLE PROSPERITY

58 WISHING FOR ABUNDANCE

60 GOOD FORTUNE

Prosperity oil

TOOLS Dropper bottle or mason jar I Funnel **INGREDIENTS** 2 tbsp base oil (almond or grapeseed) I 3 drops cinnamon oil I 3 drops peppermint oil I 3 drops honeysuckle oil I 1 bay leaf I Pinch of dried basil

Ideal for drawing either money or non-monetary prosperity to you, this oil can be used by itself or as part of a spell or ritual. It is perfect for dressing your prosperity candles, or you can use it daily to bring affluence your way. Start by cleansing your tools and ingredients (see page 27). Add each ingredient to the bottle, while speaking the words:

As the ingredients of this oil combine, may prosperity be mine. So mote it be.

Shake the bottle to activate the ingredients' energies. Pour one drop onto your hands and rub them together until warm. Move your hands over your body while saying the incantation:

May I attract good fortune and prosperity, so mote it be.

BEST TIME Waxing Moon or Full Moon
NOTE For topical use only

Prosperity tea

TOOLS Jar or container I Tea strainer **INGREDIENTS** 9 tsp green tea I 9 tsp mint leaves I 9 tsp camomile leaves I Pinch of cinnamon I 1 tsp honey (optional)

Teas and infusions are a great way to bring herbal magick into your day-to-day life. May this prosperity tea inspire you, and open doors to good fortune.

Start by cleansing your ingredients by rubbing your hands together until warm, then holding them over the ingredients and saying:

May these ingredients be cleansed and blessed.

To make your tea blend, combine the ingredients in your jar, stirring clockwise to draw whatever form of prosperity you wish to manifest towards you.

Now make your tea by adding a teaspoon of your blend to a cup and pouring boiling water over it. Strain after five minutes. Adding a teaspoon of honey will sweeten the tea as well as increasing the prosperity energy. Before drinking, say the simple incantation:

May I attract good fortune and prosperity, so mote it be.

Drink your tea mindfully, savouring the fragrant flavours and focusing on your intention.

BEST TIME Waxing Moon or Full Moon
NOTE If you're pregnant or breastfeeding, seek advice before drinking herbal teas.

Prosperity floor wash

TOOLS Bucket | Mop | Knife **INGREDIENTS** 1 whole fresh lime | 3 drops jasmine oil | 1 litre (1¾ pints) clean water

Washing your floors has numerous benefits, both mundane and metaphysical. Washing away doubt and creating a prosperous atmosphere is the goal of this spell.

Start by cutting the lime into thin slices. Add the lime and the jasmine oil to the bucket along with a litre (1¾ pints) of clean water. Let the ingredients infuse the water for 10 minutes.

Mop your floor as usual and with each sweep, visualize old stagnant energies being washed away and replaced with vibrant green and gold shimmers of light, creating an atmosphere of prosperity. Say the incantation:

*I wash away the old, for prosperity
to come my way. So mote it be.*

BEST TIME Sunday or Waxing Moon

Abundance crystal grid

TOOLS Citrine | Aventurine | Honey calcite | Pyrite | Tiger's Eye | Camomile flowers | Clover | Jasmine | Poppy (or you could use any other crystals and flowers associated with prosperity, see pages 179–183)

Crystal grids are a beautiful way to draw positive energies into your home and are a source of endless creativity. For this grid, you can use as many or as few crystals as you like – let your intuition guide you.

Start by cleansing your crystals and flowers (see page 27). Next, create a spiral pattern with them, starting from the outside moving inwards. While doing so, focus on your breathing and visualize abundance making its way to you, being drawn in by your grid in a spiral motion. When you are finished, feel the energy surrounding you and go about your day. Know that the combined energies of your ingredients and intention will draw abundance towards you. You may also sit in meditation by the grid to reaffirm your intentions.

BEST TIME Waxing Moon

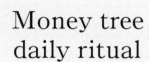

Money tree daily ritual

TOOLS Spray bottle **INGREDIENTS** Sun water (see tip)

Certain trees are associated with affluence. They require nourishment and time to grow, as does a steady influx of good fortune and prosperity. Making this ritual part of your daily routine will help draw more money to you.

Start by cleansing the spray bottle (see page 27). Add some of your sun water to the bottle. Now you need to select your tree or plant to tend. The one you choose should be associated with prosperity and money (see correspondences on page 182–185) and can be shop bought, planted yourself, or could even be a tree in your garden or favourite forest or park.

Every day, sit by your money tree and centre and ground yourself (see page 27). Meditate on money coming to you – visualize a tree with strong roots and money for leaves, in luscious gold and green colours. Each time you visit your tree, spray a little sun water on it and say the incantation:

May money grow for me as sturdy and secure as this tree, so mote it be.

———————

BEST TIME Daily or at least weekly
TIP To make sun water, leave a jar of clean water in direct sunlight from sunrise until sunset.

Prosperity bowl ritual

TOOLS Large bowl | Coins and paper money (however much you wish) **INGREDIENTS** 1 tsp basil | 1 tsp cinnamon | 1 tsp thyme | 1 Aventurine crystal tumble | 1 Pyrite crystal | 1 Citrine tumble

A prosperity bowl, often called a money bowl, is intended to keep money flowing to you. By frequently adding money to the bowl, you draw wealth to you. This is a form of representational magick. An important part of any bowl spell is to keep things moving to symbolize a flow, so remove items from your bowl and add new things every once in a while.

Start by cleansing your bowl and ingredients (see page 27). Then, one by one, layer in the basil, cinnamon, and thyme, mixing them with your finger and stating your intention for each ingredient. In a triangle (thought to be a shape to capture energies), add each crystal, once again stating your intentions. Next, place the money into your bowl, right in the centre of the crystal triangle, and say the incantation:

Money flows my way, may it come may it come! So mote it be.

Place this bowl on your altar or in your room somewhere you can easily see it, and frequently add money and other money-corresponding tokens to it over time to keep the energy flowing. If the bowl starts to overflow, it is time to take out the older money and tokens, cleanse them with incense, and tuck them away for later use.

———————

BEST TIME Full Moon

Prosperity jar

TOOLS Small glass jar | Small funnel | Lighter or matches | Pen or pencil | Green or yellow/golden chime candle (or a hot glue gun with green, golden, or yellow glue) **INGREDIENTS** ½ tsp basil | ½ tsp clover | ½ tsp cinnamon | ½ tsp mint | 1 piece dried and crushed lemon peel | Chips of crystals associated with prosperity (see page 179) | 1 bay leaf

Jar spells are an excellent way to draw in energy and keep it contained. They work slowly and steadily, making them perfect for attracting a steady flow of money.

Start by cleansing your glass jar (see page 27). Layer in the basil, clover, cinnamon, mint, lemon peel, and the crystal chips. On your bay leaf write the word "prosperity" and add it to the jar. Close the jar, and seal it by dripping candle wax around the lid, or alternatively use the hot glue gun.

You can speak a simple affirmation into the jar. You could either choose your words intuitively, or say:

May money be drawn to this jar, may it grow and flow, so mote it be.

Shake every so often to activate the energies of the spell jar, and whenever you feel in need of some extra prosperity.

Decide on an appropriate place to keep your jar – it should be somewhere you associate with prosperity-related matters, such as on a shelf next to your finance folders, or close to wherever you keep your wallet or purse.

BEST TIME Saturday, Sunday, Thursday, Waning Moon or New Moon

Money candle spell

TOOLS Green or gold candle, tea light, or chime | Carving tool | Cauldron | Lighter or matches | Pen | Fireproof plate | 1 fake currency note (drawn, printed, or shop bought) **INGREDIENTS** 3 drops prosperity oil (see page 47) | A few leaves of dried mint or 1 tsp powdered dried mint | ½ tsp cinnamon | Salt

You can perform this spell weekly, or whenever needed, to manifest extra money. As you are using fire, the results should be quicker, making this spell ideal if you need money to come to you in a timely manner. Casting a circle of protection is recommended (see page 26).

Cleanse yourself, your space, your tools, and the ingredients, and ground and centre yourself (see pages 26-27). Start by tapping the candle on your altar or workspace to "wake it".

Carve a prosperity sigil or the rune Fehu (see pages 21-22) into your candle. Dress the candle with the prosperity oil by pouring some of it onto your hands and then wiping your fingers over the candle from both ends, until your fingers touch in the middle. This is to represent drawing in money. Then sprinkle the dried mint and cinnamon over the candle, place the candle on your plate, and sprinkle a salt circle around it.

Next, take your fake money and write these words on it:

> *Money easily comes my way, and*
> *long shall it stay, so mote it be.*

Speak the words out loud while writing. Now light your candle and burn the 'currency', dropping it into your cauldron. Focusing on the flame, visualize money coming to you. Meditate for a few minutes, or until the candle has burned down completely, and then open the circle.

BEST TIME Sunday, Waxing or Full Moon
Around midsummer

Prosperity witch ladder

TOOLS 3 equal lengths of cord (colour corresponding, see page 177) | Your own hair, or personal item | 3 green beads and 3 gold beads (glass or plastic) | 3 bells | 3 feathers | Other prosperity-related tokens of your choosing

You can create a witch ladder by plaiting three cords together, making knots, and weaving in tokens of a specific intent.

Start by casting a circle and grounding and centring. Cleanse your altar space and the tools (see page 27). Make a base knot to start your braid. Begin plaiting the cords, being mindful of your intention, visualizing it the entire time. Incorporate your hair or personal item, tie a knot, and continue plaiting. Continue to add each of the beads, bells, and other tokens. For each knot you make, speak the chant below, until you have woven them all in and reach the end of the cord:

> *By the first knot, let the spell begin,*
> *By the second knot, let the magick rise,*
> *By the third knot, I weave together,*
> *By the fourth knot, may it hold strong,*
> *By the fifth knot, I speak to create,*
> *By the sixth knot, I create to change,*
> *By the seventh knot, the future is set,*
> *By the eighth knot, my will is done.*

Seal your witch ladder with a final knot and say:

> *By the ninth knot, I have spoken, may*
> *my will come true, so mote it be.*

Hang this witch ladder near your altar, in your office, or in a place that symbolizes money to you.

BEST TIME Friday or Sunday, Full Moon or Waxing Moon

Enchanted wallet spell

TOOLS 1 tea light candle | 1 incense stick | Lighter or matches | 1 bowl of sun water (see tip page 49) | 1 bowl of soil | Your wallet or purse | Pen **INGREDIENTS** 1 bay leaf

Your wallet or purse both represents and symbolizes money and prosperity. This spell enchants your wallet so it attracts more money, while also keeping you from spending too much.

Ground and centre yourself, and cast a circle (see pages 26–27). Cleanse your tools and the bay leaf by rubbing your hands together until warm, then holding them over the bay leaf and saying:

May these ingredients be cleansed and blessed.

Light the candle and the incense. Place each elemental tool – the bowl of water, the soil, the candle, and the incense – in a circle, located in the appropriate cardinal direction (see below), depending on your location (you can use your phone's compass to work those out) – the bowl of sun water (representing the element of water) to your west, the soil (representing the element of earth) to the north, the candle (representing fire) to the south, and the incense (representing air) to the east. Now take your wallet or purse, hold it over the bowl of soil, then over the incense, the candle, and the bowl of water, visualizing the elemental properties of each of these tools permeating it (see page 182 for elemental correspondences). As you do this, be sure to thank each element for its blessings.

Finally, place your wallet in the centre of your circle of tools, take the bay leaf and draw your money sigil (see page 22) on it with the pen. Then tuck the bay leaf into your wallet, where it should be kept. When finished, open the circle.

BEST TIME New Moon

Money sigil spell

TOOLS Pen | Paper | Cauldron | Lighter or matches

To quickly draw money to you, create a sigil of prosperity and abundance. This sigil can be used by itself, drawn on your body or an amulet, or as part of a spell or ritual.

Start by casting a circle, grounding and centring, and cleansing your altar space and the tools (see pages 26–27). Create a sigil for money (see page 22) and write this sigil on the piece of paper. Fold it three times towards you, turning it clockwise to invoke. Speak the incantation:

Money, money comes my way, quick as fire, however much I now require. So mote it be.

Activate the sigil by lighting the paper and burning it in the cauldron. When you've finished, open your circle.

_____

BEST TIME Waxing Moon

Charming a coin spell

TOOLS A coin

This simple spell results in a charmed coin that you can carry with you in your wallet or purse to draw in extra money – just make sure you mark this coin somehow so you don't accidentally spend it. Using a currency you don't usually have could be a good idea.

Start by rubbing your hands together until they are warm. Now take your coin and hold it between your hands as if in prayer. Feel the coin warming up with your energy. Using visualization let your energy and that of the universe flow into the coin until the coin feels heavy. Then speak the words:

May this coin be cleansed and blessed, and may it bring me money at my request. So mote it be.

Place this coin in your wallet or purse, being careful not to spend it unintentionally. Spend the coin on something important and imagine the coin entering the world to pass on prosperity to all who encounter it.

_____

BEST TIME Waxing Moon

Walnut prosperity spell

TOOLS Small piece of paper | Pen | Natural thread or twine | Shovel
INGREDIENTS 1 whole walnut

Walnuts are associated with prosperity and good fortune, as well as protection. This simple spell is best performed outside, and will assist in growing and protecting your money by a specific value.

Start by grounding and centring, and cleansing your tools and the walnut (see pages 26–27). Break open the walnut carefully, so the shell halves stay intact. Put the fruit aside for a later spell or eat it. On the piece of paper, write how much money you wish to come your way, remembering to stay humble. If you don't wish to manifest a certain amount, simply draw your money sigil or the rune Fehu (see pages 21–22) on the paper. Tuck the paper into one of the walnut shells and close both halves. Wrap the thread around them to close the walnut. Bury the walnut and say the words:

So mote it be.

———————

BEST TIME Full or Waxing Moon

Abundance charm bag

TOOLS Cotton or linen pouch or piece of cloth | Green or gold pen or thread | Needle | Green or gold string **INGREDIENTS** 3 coins of your currency | 3 bay leaves | 3 basil leaves | 1 small prosperity crystal (Aventurine or Pyrite) | 1 cinnamon stick or ½ tsp ground cinnamon | Prosperity oil (see page 47)

This fragrant charm bag will draw abundance and riches to you. Treasure it and keep it in your bag or purse, or wherever you keep your money.

Start by casting a circle, grounding and centring, and cleansing your tools and altar space (see pages 26–27). Take your pouch or cloth and draw or sew on your sigil of prosperity or the rune Fehu (see pages 21–22). Now add your dry ingredients to the pouch or cloth. Pour three drops of the prosperity oil on top. Speak into the opening of the pouch:

May this pouch collect for me,
Money and prosperity,
So mote it be.

Now fully tie together your charm bag. Then open the circle.

———————

BEST TIME Waxing Moon or Full Moon, Friday or Sunday

Ocean wishing spell

TOOLS Wooden stick | A small offering for the waves (something biodegradable and non-toxic to animals)

We know how soothing watching waves can be and in this spell the sea will take on symbolic resonance, the waves carrying away a wish to be granted.

On the evening of a Full Moon, when the moon has already risen, go to the beach or nearby body of water and take a walk, or sit in the sand or on the ground. Your feet should be bare, to feel the earth beneath you and connect to nature. When you're in a calm, happy state, start your spell by taking the stick and moving to where the water meets the land. In the sand or earth, write your wish, focusing on your intention. Stand facing the water, and watch it lap over your wish in the sand or earth. Speak the words:

Mighty water, you have given us life, may you grant this wish I have. In return I offer you [your offering], to show my thanks and appreciation. So mote it be.

Throw your offering into the water and watch it get carried away – the offering could be as simple as some flowers you grew, or a beautifully carved piece of wood. At this point, sit down and raise your energy, and try to feel the energy of the body of water in front of you. Visualize yourself with your wish already fulfilled, all the joy you will feel, and the things you plan on doing. Thank the water before leaving.

BEST TIME Full Moon

A simple wishing candle

TOOLS Pen | Tea light candle | Lighter or matches | Cauldron or fireproof container **INGREDIENTS** 1 bay leaf

This spell involves sitting with your intentions and desires. It is quick to perform and doesn't require many ingredients, making it an excellent spell for beginners.

Start by casting a circle, grounding and centring, and cleansing your altar space and the tools (see pages 26–27). Next, on the bay leaf write a word or sentence describing what you wish to manifest. Light the candle and burn the bay leaf and drop it into the cauldron. Sit in meditation and visualize your wish manifesting. When you've finished, open the circle.

BEST TIME Waxing Moon or Full Moon

A wishbone talisman

INGREDIENTS 1 whole chicken or turkey | 1 bowl of sun water (see tip, page 49) | 1 small pouch | 1 tsp basil | 1 tsp mint | 1 crushed walnut

Using bones has long been a part of witchcraft in several cultures, and has even made its way into our modern day mainstream beliefs and practices. Using a wishbone to make a wish at the dinner table has become so commonplace that few people would associate it with witchcraft. Ideally, you would cast this spell on a day that you would usually make a big chicken or turkey roast, though you could combine this spell with your own celebration if you would prefer not to have to wait for the next seasonal festivities.

It's best to carry out this spell in the kitchen. Clean the chicken or turkey as you normally would and find the wishbone, which is located between the neck and breast of the bird, and remove it. Once you have removed the bone, place it in a bowl of sun water to wash it and infuse it with some extra prosperity energy. Once it is clean, leave it to dry completely.

In the pouch, add the basil, mint, crushed walnut, and your wishbone. Whisper into the pouch any wish you may have and then close it. Carry this pouch with you until your wish is fulfilled, or, hang it near your altar. Prepare your chicken or turkey as you normally would, and enjoy your dinner while focusing on good fortune, gratitude, and a hopeful future.

BEST TIME Thursday or Sunday, New Moon or Waxing Moon
TIP If you do not eat meat, you could use a branch that resembles a wishbone.

Bring in the light fire

TOOLS Piece of cotton fabric, roughly 10 x 10cm (4 x 4in) | Thread or twine | Glass prayer candle | Lighter or matches
INGREDIENTS 1 tsp basil | 1 tsp cinnamon

This spell is inspired by the Baltic folk practice of building a bonfire, keeping the fire alive all night, and jumping over it to cleanse yourself and bring in good fortune for the next year. In this spell, you will craft a doll to represent yourself.

Start by casting a circle, grounding and centring, and cleansing your altar space and tools (see pages 26-27). Then take the piece of cotton and in the centre add a teaspoon of the basil. Take the ends of the cotton, lifting it up, and with your thumb and index finger, secure the herb bundle so that you can easily tie the thread or twine around the herbs to create the "head". Once secured, cut the ends of the thread and open the cotton to add the cinnamon "body", again tying it together. Once the doll is complete, lick your thumb and press it against the face to bind the doll to you. Light the candle and visualize blessings coming your way. Take your doll and move it from the left side of the candle, over the flame, to the right side, representing you jumping over the fire to cleanse yourself. Once done, open the circle.

Both the lit candle and the doll should stay on your altar overnight, so it carries the sunlight over from one day to the next. Let the candle burn until completely spent, and place your doll somewhere safe.

Keep the doll until the next year and burn it then to be replaced with a new doll. As it burns, visualize a cleansing and a releasing of the old, clearing space for new things to enter into your life.

BEST TIME Evening, when the sun is still up

Lucky horseshoe candle spell

TOOLS 1 tea light candle | Lighter or matches | 1 horseshoe (real, or drawn and cut out from paper) | Fireproof plate | Knife **INGREDIENTS** 1 apple | 3 clovers (preferably four-leaf)

Horseshoes have long been associated with luck and money, and many households would have had an upright horseshoe hanging above their front door to "catch good fortune". This spell is inspired by that tradition.

Ground and centre yourself, and cast a circle. Cleanse all your tools and ingredients (see page 27) and place the plate on your altar. Hold the apple and the horseshoe in your hands, and visualize a circuit of energy flowing from the Earth below you, the universe above you, and your own energy, charging them with your intent. Place the horseshoe on the plate, facing upwards so it looks like a U. Then take the knife and cut the apple horizontally (not through the stem) so that you have two halves. Notice that the apple seeds form a pentagram. Place one half of the apple on the plate in the horseshoe (you may need to cut a flat "base" so it sits firmly), and eat the other half, taking in the properties of the apple.

Place the tea light candle on the apple half sitting on the plate, and position the clovers in a triangle shape around the horseshoe and apple. Light your candle and while the flame burns, visualize luck coming your way. Meditate until the candle burns out or you feel the energy has been released, and open the circle.

Now hang the horseshoe above your door, again so it is positioned upwards, like the letter U.

BEST TIME Thursday, Waxing Moon

PERSONAL GROWTH

SPELLS

A beautiful aspect of witchcraft is its capacity to be used for personal growth, from increasing confidence and working on flaws, to revealing a version of yourself that would make your younger self look on with awe.

65 SELF-REALIZATION AND EMPOWERMENT

68 INTUITION

70 SELF-LOVE AND BEAUTY

74 SELF-REFLECTION

78 DAILY GROWTH

Empowerment oil

TOOLS Dropper bottle or mason jar **INGREDIENTS** 2 tbsp base oil (almond or grapeseed) | 3 drops rosemary oil | 3 drops verbena oil | 3 drops milk thistle oil | 3 Tiger's Eye crystal chips

This oil is intended to give you the strength to create your own reality. It can be used by itself or as an ingredient in other spells or rituals, and is perfect for dressing your candles.

Start by cleansing your ingredients (see page 27). Add each ingredient to the bottle, while saying:

With each ingredient that I add, the powers come together, I am strong, I am empowered, I am free, so mote it be.

Shake the bottle or jar to activate the ingredients' energies. Pour one drop of the oil onto your hands and rub them together until warm. Pull your hands apart slightly, feeling the energy, then move your hands towards your chest, as if to push that energy into your own heart. Say the incantation:

I am strong, I am empowered, I am free, so mote it be.

BEST TIME Waxing Moon or Full Moon
NOTE For topical use only

Personal growth sigil

TOOLS Pen | Paper | Body lotion

To assist in your personal growth journey, create a sigil that you can draw on your skin. Use this in a spell or as part of your daily ritual.

Start by cleansing your altar space and the tools (see page 27). To create a sigil for personal growth, write either the words "personal growth" or more specific goals or affirmations. Use the technique outlined on page 22 to create your sigil.

To activate your sigil, draw it on your body with lotion, so it may work over time.

BEST TIME Waxing Moon

A self-dedication ritual

TOOLS A token such as jewellery to commemorate this ritual

This ceremonial ritual should be carried out when you wish to dedicate yourself to the path of witchcraft. Inspired by traditional occult ceremonies, it is similar in nature to an initiation, but keep in mind this is not mandatory in the practice of witchcraft.

Cast a circle (see page 26) and sit in meditation, feeling energy flow through you. Take your token in your hands, move to the north and say the words:

Guardian of the north, element of earth, infuse my token with your strength.

Then move to the east and say:

Guardian of the east, element of air, infuse my token with your wisdom.

Next move to the south and say:

Guardian of the south, element of fire, infuse my token with your courage.

Lastly move to the west and say:

Guardian of the west, element of water, infuse my token with your healing energies.

Stand in the centre of the circle you have just created and place your hands over your heart, feeling the energy there.

Then slowly raise your hands, expanding the energy to flow freely upwards. Say the words:

Divine energy, I come today to dedicate myself to the path of witchcraft, to learning and growing evermore, to accepting and loving, and to appreciating the magick within us and around us. So I swear this oath, so mote it be.

Now hold your token and kiss it. Either sit in meditation, or feast with the spirits present. When finished, release the spirits by walking the circle anticlockwise, thanking each spirit, and then open the circle.

BEST TIME Whenever you feel ready, pick a special day, such as a Full Moon, seasonal celebrations, or a birthday.

Empowerment candle

TOOLS Cauldron or fireproof bowl | 1 white candle | Lighter or matches **INGREDIENTS** 1 tsp rosemary | 1 tsp vervain | 1 tsp thyme | 5 fresh carnations | 5 bay leaves

Perhaps you need to summon some inner courage to move forwards or overcome a hurdle. Perform this spell whenever you wish to bring an essence of strength, confidence, independence, and empowerment into your life.

Centre and ground yourself and cast a circle. Cleanse your tools and ingredients (see pages 26–27). Place your cauldron in the centre of your altar and position your candle in the middle. Now sprinkle the rosemary, vervain, and thyme in a circle around the candle, clockwise to draw energy towards you.

Visualize and focus on strength, courage, and empowerment, envisioning what colours they may be. Next, place the carnations around the candle in a wider circle, creating the five points of a pentagram. Place the bay leaves in the gaps between the carnations to complete the pentagram. Now light your candle, and speak the incantation:

I call upon the four elements,
I call upon the plant spirits,
assist me in this spell,
may I create for myself what I desire,
may I be courageous, and strong,
and empowered. So mote it be.

Sit in meditation until the candle has burned out. As you watch the flame, focus on your intention and envision yourself absorbing strength.

Once finished, open the circle. The leftover herbs and flowers can either be added to an empowerment jar, or buried in your garden or a pot plant.

───────

BEST TIME Full Moon

Psychic enhancement tea

TOOLS Jar or container | Tea strainer **INGREDIENTS** 3 tsp dried honeysuckle | 3 tsp dried hibiscus | 3 tsp dried peppermint | 3 tsp dried mugwort

Teas and herbal infusions have long been used to tap into the psychic realm, either through the process of ritual, meditation, trance, or using hallucinogenic ingredients. This tea is not hallucinogenic, but it will enhance your psychic abilities.

Combine all ingredients in your jar and hold your hands above the mixture, raising energy and visualizing a purple silvery light surrounding the blend, enhancing the properties and charging it with your intent. To make the tea, add a teaspoon of the blend to a cup, pour boiling water over, and strain after five minutes. Before drinking say:

May this blend enhance my psychic abilities, let me sense beyond the ordinary, so mote it be.

BEST TIME Full Moon
NOTE It is unsafe to ingest mugwort when pregnant.

Psychic charm bag

TOOLS Cotton or linen pouch | Purple or silver pen or thread | A needle (if using thread) | Purple or silver string **INGREDIENTS** 1 twig of cedar | 3 dried rowan berries | 1 tsp dried mugwort | 1 Amethyst tumble | 1 Moonstone tumble

This charm bag is intended to enhance your psychic abilities over time. Carry it with you or keep it under your pillow.

Start by casting a circle, grounding and centring, and cleansing your tools (see pages 26-27). Take the pouch and draw or sew on a sigil of psychic enhancement (see page 22) or the rune Perthro (see page 21). Now add all the ingredients to the pouch. Loosely tie the top of it together, but not yet fully.

Speak into the small opening of the pouch:

May this pouch enhance my psychic abilities and clairvoyancy, to see, hear, taste, smell, and feel what is around me but I do not yet perceive, so mote it be."

Now fully tie together your charm bag and open the circle.

BEST TIME Waxing Moon or Full Moon

More confidence sigil

INGREDIENTS Empowerment oil (see page 65) or body lotion

This is a great ritual if you have a big day ahead. Perhaps there's an important event on your horizon that requires a boost of self-confidence. Or make this part of your daily self-care routine if you regularly find yourself lacking in confidence.

Prepare for this spell by creating a sigil of confidence (see page 22).

When you have a shower in the morning, take five minutes to close your eyes and imagine the water cleansing you, removing any fear or doubt you may have. Envision the water emitting bright sunny colours and showering you with the warmth and strength of the sun. Let it soak into your skin and say the words:

As the warmth touches my skin, may it soak in, and I will shine with confidence from within, so mote it be.

After showering, use the empowerment oil or a body lotion to draw your sigil on your stomach.

———————

BEST TIME In the morning

TIP If you can, take the shower when the sun is rising, to harness its powers.

Glamour box ritual

TOOLS A small to medium-size box

INGREDIENTS 1 handful pink salt I 1 handful dried rose petals

You can cast glamour spells to intentionally create an illusion, so you appear a certain way to the outside world in order to achieve your desires. This is the perfect little charging box for your daily glamours.

Start by cleansing your ingredients (see page 27). Now add the salt to the box, and then place the rose petals on top. Say the words:

May all that be placed inside this box be enchanted to bring out my inner beauty whenever I wear them.

Add any jewellery or makeup, to this box that you wish to charge up for a glamour – such as a necklace to appear extra attractive for a special date.

———————

BEST TIME Wednesday, Full Moon

Self-love bowl

TOOLS Large bowl | Incense **INGREDIENTS** 1 tsp basil | 1 tsp cinnamon | 1 tsp thyme | 1 Rose Quartz crystal | 1 Moonstone crystal | Any items you associate with self-love

Perfect for enhancing your sense of self-worth and reminding you of your sparkling brilliance, this self-love bowl should have constant flow, so regularly feed it with tokens that represent self-love to you.

Start by cleansing your bowl and ingredients (see page 27). Then, one by one, layer in the basil, cinnamon, and thyme, mixing them with your finger, and stating your intention for each ingredient. Next, add both crystals, once again stating your intentions and any other tokens that remind you of self-love to the bowl. Say the incantation:

Self-love I sow, may you grow.
Let the energies flow in,
reminding me of how precious and worthy I am.
So mote it be.

Place this bowl on your altar or in your bedroom, preferably in a place where you get ready, and add tokens to it over time to keep the energy flowing. If the bowl starts to overflow, it is time to take out the older tokens, cleanse them with incense (see page 27), and tuck them away for later use.

BEST TIME Full Moon or Waxing Moon

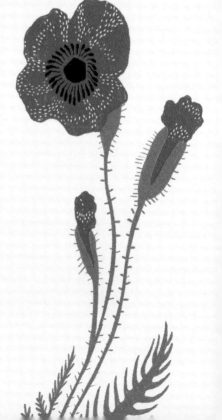

Self-love bath spell

TOOLS Candles for ambience (optional) Lighter or matches (optional) **INGREDIENTS** 120ml (4fl oz) Full Moon water (see tip page 34) | 245g (8¾oz) Epsom salt | 1 large handful dried rose petals | 1 apple, sliced | 4 drops vanilla essential oil | Your favourite fresh flowers

This soothing bath is the perfect end to a day of self-care, ideally following some hearty cooking and a good book. Simply lie back and relax, feeling nurtured, loved, and supported.

Draw your water, light your candles, and add your ingredients to the water with intent, one by one. Sink into your bath and take several deep breaths. Focus on relaxing each of your body parts while your eyes are closed, and feel the enveloping sensation of the water around you. Breathe deeply and inhale the scents arising from your beautifully fragranced bath. Let the warm water cradle you, supporting your limbs and soothing your soul.

Once you feel fully soaked, collect the apple slices and other ingredients to gently rub over your body so that they may soak up any old energy fully and completely. If you feel comfortable, this bath is also an excellent opportunity to practise some sacred sensuality and sexual self-love, using the climax to intentionally focus on a self-love goal. Visualize the energy of your climax being directed and targeted towards this personal goal.

BEST TIME Sunset, Friday, Full Moon

Shadow work ritual

TOOLS Black candle | Lighter or matches | Tarot deck | Journal | Pen

Your shadow self is the dark side of your personality, a part of you that is hard to get to know as it means exploring personal traumas and uncomfortable truths. This spell is intended to get you started on your shadow work journey, to help you heal from within.

Start by casting a circle, grounding and centring, then cleansing your altar space and tools (see pages 26–27). Next, ask any spirits, allies, deities, or ancestors you may work with to join you for this spell, as they may be able to assist you. Light the candle, and shuffle your tarot cards, reciting:

Cards, show me what I may not like, but need to see about myself, so I may grow and accept myself. So mote it be.

Lay out a three-card spread starting with the centre, and then place one card to its left and one to the right. The centre card represents you in that moment and how you see yourself. The card on the left symbolizes a behaviour in your past that you have not yet acknowledged, and the card on the right shows what work you need to do to truly accept your shadow self. Take your time with this spread and feel free to pull extra clarification cards. Use your journal to write detailed notes on your interpretations and how these cards make you feel.

Now write down your traits or traumas that you wish to work on. Rip out the page, fold it, and place it beneath the candle. This is the first step to acknowledging your shadows. When finished, extinguish the candle, thank and release your spirits, and open the circle.

BEST TIME New Moon, Monday

26–27). Ask any spirits, allies, deities, or ancestors you may work with to join you for this spell to guide you. Next, take your bowl of water and place it on your altar. Sit in a comfortable position facing the bowl. Gaze into the water and say:

Water, water, reveal to me my true self,
may I see and may I accept what you
show to me, so mote it be.

Look upon your reflection and meditate on what your shadow self is truly like, consider that it has always been a part of you, and that is okay. Take the paper from the "Shadow work ritual", unfold it, and read the words you previously wrote. Then, place the paper in the bowl of water and, with your dominant hand, stir the water and paper, clockwise to signify accepting your shadows, until it disintegrates. Say the words:

Water, strong and soothing, take my shadows
and cleanse them with your essence.

As the paper disintegrates, focus on your shadows and your own reflection blending together, and accept that you cannot separate yourself from them; they are a part of who you are. Then take your time to write in your journal, and try talking to your shadow self, acknowledging its presence and how it has affected your life and personality. Explore where it shows up in your life most. How has it blended in with who you think you are? Where has it trickled into your daily habits? When finished, thank and release your spirits and open the circle. Pour the water away or use it in another shadow work spell.

BEST TIME New Moon, Monday

Accepting your shadows ritual

TOOLS Bowl of water | Journal | Pen

As hard as it can be to get to know your shadow self – your triggers and any uncomfortable truths – it can be even harder to accept them fully. This spell should be performed after the "Shadow work ritual" opposite and is intended to assist you further in this journey of self-discovery and true acceptance.

Start by casting a circle, grounding and centring, and cleansing your altar space and tools (see pages

Forgiving yourself ritual

TOOLS Incense | Lighter or matches | Pen | Paper | Thread

This spell should be performed only after you have carried out the "Shadow work ritual" and the "Accepting your shadows ritual" (see pages 74-75). This ritual represents the next step in your journey to embodying your shadow self – you will cast a spell of forgiveness to yourself.

Start by casting a circle, grounding and centring, and cleansing your altar space and tools (see pages 26-27). Ask any spirits, allies, deities, or ancestors you may work with to join you, as they may be able to support you. Light the incense and gather your pen and paper. Now take your time to write a letter of forgiveness to yourself. Be as honest as possible, letting out any past traumas you have buried, hurtful or embarrassing situations, embarrassing encounters,

any circumstances you would prefer to forget, and forgive yourself. When you have finished writing the letter, fold it in half towards you, to call forgiveness to yourself, and wrap the thread around it to form a cross. Tie a knot, and while doing so, speak the words:

The spell is done, I tie it in, forgiveness may come, so mote it be.

Next, hold your letter in the incense smoke so that your intentions may be carried away to the wind. When you've finished, thank and release your spirits and open the circle. Keep the letter safely hidden – you can use it for the "Releasing the past" spell (opposite).

_____

BEST TIME New Moon, Monday

Releasing the past

TOOLS Pen | Paper, or your letter from the "Forgiving yourself ritual" (opposite) | Cauldron or fireproof container | Lighter or matches

This spell is intended to support your personal growth by helping to release the past, letting go of any hurt emotions, trauma, sadness, or anger - especially those you direct inwardly.

Start by casting a circle, grounding and centring, and cleansing your altar space and tools (see pages 26–27). Ask any spirits, allies, deities, or ancestors you may work with to join you. On your piece of paper, write down the things you wish to let go of. Or, take your letter and sit in meditation with it, reflecting on all that you have written. Focus deeply on the emotions that arise and the things you would like to rid yourself of, so

that you may grow and continue with your life in a happier state. Now take the letter and light it, and drop it into the cauldron. As the paper burns, imagine it releasing all that was written on the letter. Watch the words burning, being cleansed by the fire, and speak the incantation:

I release these ties, may they no longer hold power over me, so mote it be.

When finished, thank and release your spirits and open the circle. Take the ashes outside, away from your home, and sprinkle them to the wind.

BEST TIME New Moon, Monday

Morning ritual

TOOLS Tea or coffee | Tarot cards | Your favourite book or music
INGREDIENTS Sun water (see tip page 49)

This ritual sets the tone for a positive day ahead.

When you wake up, take a shower and visualize the water washing away any negative or stagnant energy. Imagine any energies from past days flowing away and being neutralized by Mother Earth. Take your sun water and splash some of it on your face to promote good fortune and a happy day.

Next, drink your coffee or tea by your altar, while pulling a tarot card, reading a book, or listening to uplifting music.

Then take 10 minutes to meditate. Meditating is one of the best ways to keep your spiritual wards up and practise energy workings, plus it will help you to visualize and manifest.

If you work with deities, spirits, or your ancestors, leave an offering for them on your altar or out in nature, thanking them for this day. Finally, ground and centre before starting the rest of your day.

BEST TIME Morning

PERSONAL GROWTH

Intentional coffee or tea daily ritual

Add a layer of depth to your morning herbal tea or coffee through knowledge of your ingredients (see correspondences pages 182-185) and by adding each of them with intention.

Stir clockwise to draw things towards you and to promote good fortune and blessings. Next, stir anticlockwise to banish and remove any unwanted energies. Scoop up any bubbles forming with your spoon and drink them to promote good fortune. To enchant your mug, rub your hands together until warm, then hold them over the mug and say:

May this mug be cleansed and blessed, prepare me for the day, so mote it be.

———————

BEST TIME Every morning

Gratitude ritual

This ritual is ideal for celebrating a Full Moon. It's also good if you are feeling down and need to lift your mood, increase your gratitude, and cultivate an attitude of contentment.

Start by casting a circle, grounding and centring, and cleansing your altar space and tools (see pages 26-27). Light your tea light candle and sit in meditation for at least five minutes. Next, write down three things that make you smile each day, followed by three things that make your life better, and lastly three things that you are simply grateful for. If you wish to write more than three things for each, feel free to do so, but try to list at least three - even if they are as simple as wearing warm socks, rewatching your favourite movie, or having a beautiful dream at night. When you have finished writing your lists, say the incantation:

I am filled with gratitude, happiness, and appreciation for all that I have. May I always remember, and may my blessings continue to come to me, so mote it be.

———————

BEST TIME Full Moon

HEALTH *and* WELLBEING

SPELLS

While they should not replace medical attention, spells such as immune-boosting teas, or folk charms for healing – both physical and emotional – can be helpful and nourishing when used in combination with traditional medicine.

81 ILLNESS BANISHMENT

84 WELLNESS AND HEALING

96 EMOTIONAL HEALTH

Tea to banish colds

TOOLS Jar or container | Tea strainer **INGREDIENTS** 1 lemon | ½ tbsp turmeric | 3 slices fresh ginger | 1 cinnamon stick | 1 tsp honey

Brew this tea to banish a cold, or to boost your immune system through winter.

Start by cleansing your ingredients (see page 27). To make the tea, boil enough water to fill your cup and wait until very warm but no longer boiling (boiling water makes the healing properties of honey ineffective). Squeeze the juice from the lemon and add all ingredients to the cup, stirring anticlockwise to banish the cold. Say this simple incantation before drinking:

May this blend banish my cold and promote good health, so mote it be.

Make each sip intentional, feeling how the warm, soothing liquid makes its way down your throat into your stomach, healing you from the inside. Visualize the tea creating a pulsing light from within, dissipating any congested energy at any affected areas, such as a sore throat.

When finishing your cup, close your eyes and take three deep breaths, giving thanks to the plants used in the tea.

———

BEST TIME Sunday, Thursday, Waning Moon
NOTE If you're pregnant or breastfeeding, seek advice before drinking herbal teas.

Absorbing potato spell

TOOLS Shovel | Plant pot | Soil **INGREDIENTS** 1 potato

This simple spell uses a potato to quickly absorb illness and promote good health.

Start by cleansing your tools and ingredients by rubbing your hands together until warm, then holding them over the ingredients and saying:

May these ingredients be cleansed and blessed.

Take your potato and slowly move it over your body, while visualizing the potato picking up any ill health. Then thank the potato, and bury it in a pot of soil or in your garden. The soil will neutralize the potato, and you will soon have a potato plant to harvest for future spells, soups, and other recipes.

———

BEST TIME Sunday, Waning Moon

Release illness knot spell

TOOLS Cord or string (natural brown or white) | Tea light candle (white) | Lighter or matches | Cauldron

The untying of knots in this spell symbolizes releasing illnesses.

Start by casting a circle and grounding and centring, and cleansing your altar space and the tools (see pages 26-27). Take the cord in your hands and meditate on your intent for a few minutes. Then begin by creating a knot at one end of the cord. You will make three knots in total - be sure not to make them too tight as you will need to reopen them again. Speak these words while tying the knots:

> *By knot of one, the spell's begun,*
> *I weave my illness into this cord,*
> *By knot of two, the magick comes true,*
> *once released, it won't return,*
> *By knot of three, so it shall be,*
> *I release all illness so mote it be.*

Once your cord has three knots in it, light your candle. Now, in reverse, open the knots again, and say the words:

> *By knot of three,*
> *may it no longer be,*
> *By knot of two, I release you,*
> *By knot of one, the spell is done,*
> *so mote it be.*

Then burn the cord using the tea light candle's flame, and drop it into the cauldron so you don't burn your fingers. Make sure the cord burns fully then open your circle.

BEST TIME Sunset, Saturday, Full Moon

Health oil

TOOLS Dropper bottle or jar | Funnel **INGREDIENTS** 3 drops rosemary oil | 3 drops ginger oil | 3 drops arnica oil | 2 drops peppermint oil | 2 tbsp base oil (almond or grapeseed)

This is perfect for candle dressing and sigil drawing to promote good health.

Start by cleansing your ingredients by rubbing your hands together until warm, then holding them over the ingredients and saying:

May these ingredients be cleansed and blessed.

Add each of the oils, apart from your base oil, to your bottle or jar. Swirl your jar to combine the oils and say the incantation:

May this oil promote good health, that which is the highest wealth, so mote it be.

Then fill the jar with the base oil. Activate the jar by shaking it before applying the oil to your body, or using it in other spells or rituals. Each time you use the oil, repeat the incantation, or let your intuition guide you on your own words.

——————————

BEST TIME Full Moon
NOTE For topical use only

Abracadabra healing amulet spell

TOOLS Paper (or a wooden disc or piece of metal) | Pen (or carving tool)

The word "Abracadabra" was used to ward off the plague, evil, and bad health. Its origin is unclear, potentially having roots in the ancient Roman empire, or Aramaic or Hebrew languages.

According to some historical accounts, people wore this type of amulet for nine days before tossing it into a river.

To make a healing amulet, write the word "Abracadabra" on the top of your paper (or carve it into your wood or metal), writing downwards to banish evil and illness like so:

Abracadabra
Abracadabr
Abracadab
Abracada
Abracad
Abraca
Abrac
Abra
Abr
Ab
A

Keep this amulet on your person for good health and protection.

─────────────

BEST TIME Full Moon, Monday

Good health bed spray recipe

TOOLS Spray bottle (glass is preferred) **INGREDIENTS** Full Moon water (see tip, page 34) | 3 drops lemon juice | 3 drops cinnamon oil | 3 drops jasmine oil | 3 drops rosemary oil

Your bed should be a place of rest and restoration. This spray is ideal to spritz around your bed to promote good health.

Add to your spray bottle the Full Moon water, lemon juice, cinnamon, jasmine, and rosemary oils, and shake well. Shaking it activates the energy as well as mixing everything together (however, oil and water will never fully combine, which is fine). Shake each time before using, and spray with intent.

Ideally spray on or around your bed half an hour or so before going to sleep. When spraying, visualize distributing healing energies around your bed and clearing away anything stagnant. You can also say the words:

This place of restoration and rest is cleansed and cleared, good health come to me, so mote it be.

─────────────

BEST TIME Full Moon

Health spell jar

TOOLS Small glass jar | Paper | Pen | 1 green candle (or hot glue gun) | Lighter or matches **INGREDIENTS** ¼ tsp of salt | ¼ tsp of peppermint | ¼ tsp rosemary | ¼ tsp lavender | 3 drops of health oil (see page 84)

Spell jars usually draw things in and contain them, in this case good health. Conduct this spell to improve your health or retain good health.

Start by cleansing your glass jar (see page 27). Layer in the salt, peppermint, rosemary, lavender, and the healing oil. On your piece of paper write your healing sigil (see spell below), or simply the words "good health", roll it up towards you, and add it to the jar. Close the jar and seal it by dripping candle wax around the lid, or alternatively use a hot glue gun. You can speak a simple affirmation into the jar. Choose your words intuitively or say:

May I stay healthy and well, protected from illness and disease, so mote it be.

Shake every so often to activate the energies of the spell jar, and whenever you are feeling unwell or need to be particularly vibrant.

———————

BEST TIME Sunday, Tuesday, Full Moon or New Moon

Good health sigil

TOOLS Pen | Paper

To bring healing and good health your way, create a sigil that you can draw on your skin, in the air above a minor wound, or use as part of another spell or ritual.

Start by cleansing your altar space and the tools. To create a sigil for good health, write either the words "physical health" – or choose a more specific goal or affirmation – on your piece of paper. Use the technique outlined on page 22 to create your sigil.

To activate your sigil, draw it on your body with a healing salve (page 93), water (for its healing properties), or in the air above your body.

———————

BEST TIME Waxing Moon

Enchanted amber amulet spell

TOOLS Amber jewellery

Amber, a solidified tree resin, is used in many cultures, often for babies to reduce pain when they are teething. People in Baltic countries (the most renowned amber is Baltic amber) use it in various folk and everyday rituals, as it is said to promote health and prosperity.

Start by rubbing your hands together until they are warm and tingly. Now take your amber jewellery, and hold it between your hands as if in prayer. Feel the amber warming up with your energy, and say the words:

May this amber be cleansed and blessed, and may it promote good health and wealth. So mote it be.

If you prefer, you can leave out "wealth" and replace it with an intuitively chosen word.

Wear this piece of jewellery daily, or whenever you are especially looking after your health.

BEST TIME New Moon or Full Moon

Clear skin glamour spell

TOOLS Bowl of fresh water | 1 tsp Full Moon water (see tip page 34) | Rose Quartz crystal or Clear Quartz crystal

This spell is aimed at helping the healing process of your skin, and is most powerful when performed every morning and evening.

Prepare a bowl of fresh water and the moon water. Hold the Quartz crystal in your hands and close your eyes, visualizing radiant energy flowing into the crystal from you, the universe above you, and nature below you. Program your crystal for the specific intent of healing your skin by speaking unto it:

Lovely crystal, I program you, may you assist in healing my skin, infuse the water with your powers, so mote it be.

Then place the crystal next to the bowl. Wash your skin with the water and visualize your skin absorbing the healing energy, making you glow from within. Imagine the water sinking into your pores and the glow radiating all around you, boosting your confidence and allowing you to see yourself in a more loving manner.

Pour the used water away and visualize it carrying away the inflammation and irritation, which will return to nature to be neutralized. Each day that you prepare your fresh bowl of water, envision nature supplying you with naturally refreshing and cleansing energies.

BEST TIME Daily for at least seven days, the week of the Full Moon

TIP Don't place crystals in your water as they can contain bacteria in their microscopic ridges.

Waning Moon bathing ritual

TOOLS Bathtub | 1 green tea light candle | 2 white tea light candles | Lighter or matches
INGREDIENTS 150g (5½oz) salt (Epsom or table) | 1 apple, sliced | 1 handful fresh peppermint leaves | 1 handful fresh or dried camomile | 1 handful fresh dandelion flowers

The Waning Moon phase aids in releasing, decreasing, and letting go of unwanted things. It is a great phase for banishing illnesses, especially in combination with water. Bathing in a natural body of water is preferable but of course not always accessible – a bathtub is just fine.

Draw your water and light the three tea light candles. Now add the salt, apple, peppermint leaves, camomile, and dandelion flowers to your bathtub, being mindful of your intentions. Sink into the bath and let the infused water soak into your skin. Make sure you are fully submerged, using your hands to spill water over your body to draw out illness and cleanse you. Say this incantation three times:

On this Waning Moon I cleanse myself, with blissful water and herbal potency, of all illness and pain, so mote it be.

Envision how the infused water draws out all stagnant energies causing you illness and pain, both physical and emotional. Visualize the apple and other ingredients acting like sponges, allowing all of that old energy to be extracted from the water.

Finally, get out of the bath and drain the water. Collect the herbs, wash them so no salt is left on them, and take them to a river or the ocean to be released – or discard in a bin.

─────────────

BEST TIME Dusk, when the moon has risen, Tuesday or Sunday

WELLNESS AND HEALING

An enchanted hair and toothbrush ritual

TOOLS Bowl of salt | Incense | Tea light candle | Lighter or matches | Bowl of water | Waterproof pen | Paper | Your toothbrush | Your hairbrush

To add magick to your daily life, enchant your toothbrush and hairbrush to promote health, protection, or anything else you'd like to invite into your life. For this specific spell, the focus is on good health.

Start by casting a circle and grounding and centring, and cleansing your altar space and the tools (see pages 26-27). Place the bowl of salt on your altar facing north, the incense facing east, the tea light candle facing south, and the bowl of water facing west. These are your elemental representations. Light the tea light candle and the incense, then take your pen and paper and draw your good health sigil (see page 86) or the rune Laguz (see page 21). Cut the sigil or rune out, shaping the paper into a circle, and place this in the centre of the elemental representations. Now, take your toothbrush, hold it over the bowl of salt, and say:

Element of earth, charge this object with healing powers.

Repeat for each element in a clockwise circle, three times in total. Then place the toothbrush on your sigil or rune paper in the centre. Say the words:

Filled with the elemental powers of earth, air, fire, and water, I invoke the powers of the spirits, fill this object with healing powers. I invoke the energies of this [sigil/rune], may you too fill this object with your healing energies.
So mote it be."

Repeat for the hairbrush. When finished, release the spirits and open the circle.

——————————

BEST TIME Waxing Moon, Full Moon

Good health soup

TOOLS 2 large saucepans | Cutting board | Knife **INGREDIENTS** | 1 tsp salt | ½ tsp black pepper | 1 vegetable or chicken stock cube | 3 chicken breasts (vegan alternative: tofu, mushrooms, seitan) | 1 onion | 2 carrots | 4 garlic cloves | 1 bay leaf | 300g (10oz) pasta (shell, letters, your favourite). Serves 4.

This is the perfect soup to boost your immune system – it's packed with nourishing ingredients and a sprinkle of magick.

Fill a pan halfway with water then put it on a high heat. Add half the salt, pepper, stock cube, and the chicken (or vegan substitute). Dice your vegetables, crush your garlic, and add them to the pan. Before adding your bay leaf, hold it in your hands, and whisper onto it:

I wish for good health.

Stir in a clockwise motion to draw good health to you. Now let it simmer on medium heat for 1½ hours. The chicken should be cooked through and the vegetables soft.

Meanwhile, fill your second pan with hot water, add salt, and cook your pasta according to the packet instructions.

Shred the chicken with two forks. Serve it, or your vegan alternative, along with the soup and pasta in bowls with intent.

———————

BEST TIME Full Moon, Monday

HEALTH AND WELLBEING

Healing salve recipe

TOOLS Small glass jar | 1 medium-size saucepan | 1 smaller pan | Spoon or whisk **INGREDIENTS** 1 tbsp beeswax | 50ml (1¾fl oz) coconut oil | 10 drops mandarin oil | 10 drops eucalyptus oil | 10 drops lavender oil | 5 drops tea tree oil | 5 drops camomile oil | 3 drops vitamin E oil.

This healing salve is great to apply to small nicks and bumps on your skin to help the healing process.

Start by cleansing your tools and ingredients (see page 27). Fill your pan halfway with water and place it on your hob, bring to the boil, then turn the heat down to low-medium. Place the smaller pan in the water and add the beeswax (beeswax should not be heated on a direct flame). When it has melted, stir in the oils slowly - first stirring anticlockwise to banish ill health, then clockwise to draw in good health. Say the incantation:

May these healing oils combine, may they heal and banish pain, so mote it be.

Transfer the liquid to your jar and let it sit to cool without the lid for several hours (screwing on the lid could cause condensation).

When applying your wax, draw sigils of good health (see page 22) and massage in slowly, visualizing the salve soaking into your skin and a golden healing light pulsing and soothing the afflicted area.

BEST TIME Full Moon, Monday, Tuesday
NOTE For topical use only

Healing candle ritual

TOOLS Cauldron or fireproof container | 1 white pillar candle | Needle, thorn, or toothpick | Lighter or matches **INGREDIENTS** 1 tsp witch hazel | 1 tsp lavender | ½ tsp mandrake root powder | 3 cloves | Health oil (see page 84)

Using fire is an excellent way to immediately activate and release energy, making it perfect for this spell, in combination with sigils and herbs, to assist and speed up the healing process.

Start by casting a circle and grounding and centring, and cleansing your altar space and the tools (see pages 26-27). Place your cauldron or the fireproof container in the centre of your altar, and sprinkle the witch hazel, lavender, and mandrake root powder in a small pile. With your finger, stir the herbs together, three times clockwise and three times anticlockwise. Then take the candle and tap it on your altar three times to wake it up. With your needle, thorn, or toothpick carve your healing sigil (see page 22) into

the candle, then dress the candle with the health oil and roll it in the herb mix, rolling towards you. Lastly, take the three cloves and push them into the top of the candle, around the wick in a triangle. Place the candle in the centre of the cauldron with the leftover herbs and light it. Say the words:

May your fire burn away all sickness, and return to me health and vitality, so mote it be.

Sit in meditation with your candle until you intuitively feel you are ready to leave. Open the circle. Every day, sit in meditation and burn the candle.

———————

BEST TIME Every day around Full Moon

Distance healing candle

TOOLS Fireproof plate | Mirror | Picture of your loved one | 1 white votive candle | Lighter or matches **INGREDIENTS** 270g (9½oz) salt | 1 tbsp rosemary | 1 tbsp peppermint | 5 garlic cloves

Knowing a loved one is ill, and not being able to bring them soup due to distance or restrictions, is never easy, so this distance healing spell aims to send them a feeling of being loved, as well as healing powers to assist with their recuperation.

Start by casting a circle and grounding and centring, and cleansing your altar space and the tools (see pages 26-27). Place the plate in the centre of your altar and the mirror behind the plate, facing you. Prop up the picture in front of the plate, facing the mirror. Take your candle and tap it three times on the altar to wake it up. Then place it in the centre of the plate. Sprinkle the salt in a circle around the mirror, picture, and plate. Sprinkle the rosemary and the peppermint around the candle in a circle, and place each garlic clove around the candle to form a pentagram. Light the candle and speak the incantation:

I invoke and send to you healing energy, may it find you peacefully, may it wrap around you warm and lovingly, so mote it be.

When finished, open the circle. Let the candle burn down.

_____

BEST TIME Waning Moon, Sunday, Tuesday

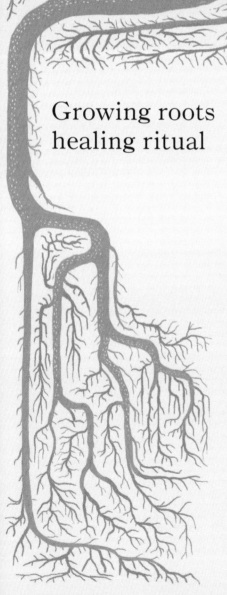

Growing roots healing ritual

TOOLS Blanket in case it is wet or cold

Nature can be soothing and restorative to the soul, especially after a difficult day, week, or year. It is so beneficial to take a day for yourself to connect to nature and just let go.

Take a walk to a secluded, safe natural location – it may be a local park, a beautiful forest, or your garden. Find a comfortable spot, possibly under a large tree that you can lean against. Sit and close your eyes, and start to ground and centre yourself. Visualize yourself growing roots, deep into the Earth, until you reach the very centre. Feel the warmth feeding back to you, filling you with bright golden or silvery light. Any stagnant, dark spot in your energy flows down to that warm bright centre, where it is neutralized, and in return you are filled with the energy of nature. It fills any fissures or cracks in your energetic field, healing you from the inside out. Say this incantation three times:

Great Mother Nature, may you take away my pain and sorrow, and fill me with your healing light. I grow roots as steady and strong as the greatest tree, may I feel its strength every morrow.
So mote it be.

When done, take three deep revitalizing breaths and give thanks to Mother Nature.

———————

BEST TIME Anytime

HEALTH AND WELLBEING

Emotional healing talisman

TOOLS Paper | Pen | Piece of natural cord or string | Small drawstring pouch
INGREDIENTS Blue Lace Agate (or alternative, see correspondences pages 180–181) | 1 tsp lavender

While the journey of emotional healing takes time and may need professional attention, this spell can call to you some extra spiritual assistance in the form of a small token to remind you how far you have already come, and to take each day at a time.

Start by casting a circle and grounding and centring, and cleansing your altar space and the tools (see pages 26-27). Take your piece of paper and pen and start writing three, six, or nine positive affirmations. They can be as simple as "I am happy" or "I am fulfilled and content". Write as if you had already attained these things. Then, place the crystal on the paper and sprinkle the lavender around it. Next, carefully lift all four corners of the paper and wrap your crystal and lavender in the paper, tying it together like a tiny parcel with the cord. Place your little parcel inside the drawstring pouch. Say the incantation:

I bless and consecrate this tool, may it now be a sacred talisman. May it be protected, and assist me in my healing journey, so mote it be.

Hold the talisman in your hands and charge it with your personal power by visualizing energy flowing from you into the pouch, until the pouch is filled to the brim - you may even feel a shift in energy or a slight buzzing in your hands. When you've finished, open the circle.

Carry this little talisman with you daily, holding it in your hands whenever needed, letting the energies flow from the pouch to you, soothing and calming your emotions.

BEST TIME Full Moon, Monday

LOVE *and* SEX

SPELLS

Spells surrounding love and sex have long been the most popular. Here you can find anything from consensual love potions and charms for better sex, to spells to help you soothe heartbreak or walk away from a lover.

99 ROMANCE

106 GLAMOUR

108 DRAWING LOVE TO YOU

112 ENDINGS AND BREAK-UPS

Romantic love oil

TOOLS Dropper bottle or roll-on bottle | Funnel **INGREDIENTS** 10 drops mandarin oil | 5 drops vanilla oil | 10 drops sandalwood oil | 3 Rose Quartz chips | Sprinkle of dried rose petals | Base oil (almond or grapeseed)

This oil is perfect to use on your skin or in spells to add a bit of romance and spice to your life. You can also use this oil in sex magick, as part of creating a romantic bond to your partner, or to invoke sensual feelings as part of a self-love ritual.

Start by cleansing your ingredients (see page 27). Add the oils, the Rose Quartz, and a sprinkle of dried rose petals to the bottle, while saying:

May this oil enhance romance and sensuality, to bring about love and passion, so mote it be.

Then fill the rest of your bottle with the base oil. Shake the bottle to activate the ingredients' energies and pour one drop onto your pressure points (wrists and neck). Visualize the oil sinking into your skin, creating a romantic energy field around you. This oil will create a scent-based reflex.

BEST TIME Friday, Full Moon
NOTE For topical use only

Rekindling the spark muffins

TOOLS 2 mixing bowls | 1 wooden spoon | Muffin tray | Paper muffin cases **INGREDIENTS** Dry: 240g (8½oz) plain flour | 170g (6oz) chocolate chips | 67g (2¼oz) sugar | A sprinkle of salt | 2 tsp baking powder | Wet: 1 tsp vanilla extract | 120ml (4fl oz) vegetable oil | 2 large eggs | 125g (4½oz) diced strawberries | 120ml (4fl oz) sweetened condensed milk

There is a saying that the way to someone's heart is through the stomach. These delicious muffins are perfect if your relationship is lacking lustre and romance and you wish to rekindle that forgotten spark.

Preheat the oven to 200°C (180°C fan/400°F/ Gas 6). Combine the wet ingredients in one bowl, and the dry ingredients in another. Do not overstir as some lumps are fine. Then fold the dry and wet together. As you combine your ingredients, say the incantation:

Strawberries for love and chocolate for lust, combine to rekindle the spark in our relationship. Rise by heat as our romance will rise again, so mote it be.

Distribute the mixture in the muffin cases and bake for 18-20 minutes or until an inserted toothpick comes out clean. Let the muffins cool for 10 minutes and serve them to your partner warm on their own, or with butter and jam.

BEST TIME Friday, Waxing Moon

Divine connection spell

TOOLS 2 pieces of jewellery | Tin box | Pen | Piece of paper | Shovel **INGREDIENTS** Red or pink rose petals | 1 Rose Quartz crystal

This spell is inspired by the tradition of gifting a piece of jewellery, often a ring, to a loved one as a symbol of the never-ending love and loyalty you share. It can be performed by both partners together, or you can give the enchanted jewellery as a special gift.

Start by casting a circle and grounding and centring, and cleansing your altar space and the tools (see pages 26–27). Now take your pieces of jewellery and hold them between your hands as if in prayer. If you are doing this with your partner, fold your hands over theirs. Feel the jewellery warming up with your energy, and say the incantation:

May this jewellery be infused with the love we have for one another, may it hold strong and true. May it connect us across continents and oceans, with love and devotion.
So mote it be.

Now take the tin box, and in it place the petals and the crystal as well as the jewellery. On the piece of paper, write the incantation once again, kiss the paper, then place it in the tin box. Once done, open the circle. Lastly, find a safe location outside (or alternatively use a pot with soil) and bury the box for nine days, to be infused by nature's energies, and to represent lasting through any storms that may arise. After the nine days, dig up the box and activate the jewellery by wearing it.

―――――――――

BEST TIME Friday, Full Moon

Lovers bath ritual

TOOLS Tea light candles for ambience | Lighter or matches **INGREDIENTS** 120ml (4fl oz) Full Moon water (see tip page 34) | 120ml (4fl oz) milk | 1 handful fresh roses (pink or red) | 1 handful fresh jasmine or hibiscus flowers | 1 apple, sliced | 3 drops romantic love oil (see page 99)

You can take this bath with your partner or alone. It is perfect as a standalone spell, or can form part of a longer ritual.

Draw your water, and one by one add your ingredients intentionally. If you wish, you can speak out loud the purpose of each ingredient (see correspondences pages 182-185). Sink into the bath together (or by yourself) and let the magick-infused water soak into your skin. Take your time to appreciate each other. Once you've finished your bath, collect all the flowers and either use for a later spell, dry them and store them, or bury them in your garden or in a pot plant.

─────────────

BEST TIME Dawn, Friday, Full Moon

Better sex pillow pouch

TOOLS A cotton or linen pouch or piece of cloth **INGREDIENTS** 2 rose petals | 2 jasmine flowers | 2 pieces Rose Quartz | 2 slices dried apple | 2 drops romantic love oil (see page 99)

Create this pouch to place under your or your lover's pillow to enhance your sex life and bring more romance and passion to your relationship.

Start by casting a circle and grounding and centring, and cleansing your altar space and the tools (see pages 26-27). Take your piece of cloth or pouch and add your rose petals, jasmine flowers, Rose Quartz, and apple. Add 2 drops of the romantic love oil onto the other ingredients and tie the pouch together, but not yet fully. Speak into the small opening of the pouch:

May this pouch bring to us passion and intimacy. So mote it be.

Now fully tie together your charm bag and then open the circle.

─────────────

BEST TIME Friday, Full Moon
TIP You could create two of these to be placed under both your and your lover's pillows.

Blessed garter charm

TOOLS Plate or flat mirror | Your garter **INGREDIENTS** 8 jasmine flowers | 8 pink roses (or petals) | 8 raspberry leaves

To prepare for your wedding day, enchant your garter (or your partner's) to promote everlasting love, passion, and compassion in your relationship.

Cleanse your plate or mirror, garter, and ingredients (see pages 26-27) and then sit in meditation with the garter for a few minutes, visualizing an energy circuit from the universe and the Earth flowing through you into the garter. Then, on the plate or mirror, place the garter, and one by one lay the jasmine flowers, pink roses, and the raspberry leaves around the garter, so they create an alternating pattern. The figure 8 stands for infinity, but you can use any number that has a special meaning to you. See the correspondences on pages 182-185 for alternative flowers if needed. Speak the words:

May this garter be blessed in love and happiness, let the love slip onto me/my partner when worn, and make the day a magickal one steeped in love and devotion.
So mote it be.

Let the garter sit in the circle of flowers overnight, or for several hours at least, to soak up the energies. When wearing the garter, visualize the energy flowing into you. Keep this garter long after the wedding by framing it, or maybe incorporate it in spells or use it in other creative magickal projects.

BEST TIME Friday, Waning Moon, Full Moon

Tying the knot love spell

TOOLS Thick piece of rope or woven cloth

Tying the knot refers to a pagan handfasting ceremony, similar to a wedding in nature. You can perform this spell prior to your wedding, or with your partner outside a wedding-related setting, simply to promise yourselves to one another.

Prepare your cord by cleansing it (see page 27). Sit together in a location that's special to you both. Start by holding each other's hands, and speak the words:

As a symbol of union we hold hands, to promise each other endless love and respect. May we give each other strength and peace, trust and honour, romance and consolation. As we join our hands, we join our lives.

Now, with your other hands, start wrapping the cord around your joined wrists and hands loosely. At this point, exchange any special vows that you have written for each other. Once done, tie both ends of the cord together below your wrists, making sure the cord is loose enough so you are able to remove your hands afterwards. Take one last moment to enjoy and feel each other's connected hands, and feel free to kiss to finalize the ceremony. Speak the words:

Blessed is this union, protected by the gods/spirits, may we walk this life together until death shall us part, to reunite in spirit once more. So mote it be.

Then remove your hands from the cord, making sure the knot is tied securely. If you are repeating an officiated handfasting at a later time, you can reuse this cord, by blessing it and opening the knot, but affirming that the untying of the knot is not to release the spell, but that it will be retied.

BEST TIME Friday, Full Moon

Lipstick enchantment

TOOLS A plate | A small bowl or glass | Red or pink lipstick (or lip balm if you prefer) | 1 red or pink candle | Lighter or matches **INGREDIENTS** 120ml (4fl oz) water | 1 tsp maple syrup | 1 tsp of sugar | 1 peach, sliced

Enchant a lipstick or lip balm to create glamour magick, with the intent of love, beauty, and divine attraction – perfect for a date or whenever you would like to feel especially charming.

Start by cleansing your ingredients by rubbing your hands together until warm, then holding them over the ingredients and saying:

May these ingredients be cleansed and blessed.

Take the plate and place the glass or bowl in the centre and pour the water onto the plate carefully. Next, add the syrup and sugar to the water and mix it clockwise with a finger on your dominant hand or a spoon. Then place the peach slices around the bowl or glass. Light the candle and hold the lipstick in both hands. Start raising energy, by visualizing or humming, focusing that energy on your lipstick. Say the incantation:

I enchant this lipstick/lip balm with divine beauty in mind, accentuate my features and bring focus to my charm, so mote it be.

Then place the lipstick or lip balm in the bowl or glass. Now visualize an energy circuit from the ingredients on the plate flowing around and into the lipstick or lip balm, infusing it with their properties. Repeat the incantation, and once it feels as if the lipstick is fully charged, you can remove it and discard the maple syrup, sugar, and fruit mixture by taking it outside or even using it in a meal. Activate the spell by applying the lipstick or lip balm.

BEST TIME Monday, Friday, Waxing Moon
WISDOM Glamour spells don't result in physical changes, but are projections that you create in order to make yourself appear a certain way.

Love potion

TOOLS Saucepan | Bowl | Wooden spoon | A glass | Marker pen **INGREDIENTS** 1 litre (1¾ pints) water | 1 fresh lemon, sliced | 1 handful hibiscus tea | 1 handful fresh strawberries, sliced | Sprinkle of dried lavender | 100g (3½oz) sugar

This love potion is a glamour spell, creating the illusion of charm and beauty. Feeling beautiful starts from within and may be a long journey – this potion assists in that.

Put your saucepan on the hob. Add the water, lemon, hibiscus tea, strawberries, and lavender. Bring to the boil, then turn down the heat and add the sugar. Let it simmer for five more minutes. Stir the potion clockwise to draw towards you. Say the incantation:

This love potion I create, to make me feel lovely inside and out. As I stir, charm and beauty shall it equate. So mote it be.

Next, take the glass and flip it upside down. Create a sigil of love and beauty (see page 22), and then copy that sigil onto the bottom of the glass with the marker pen. Serve warm as a brew, or over ice as a refreshing beverage, visualizing a bright light growing from within.

BEST TIME Friday, Waning Moon, Full Moon
NOTE If you're pregnant or breastfeeding, seek advice before drinking herbal teas.

Dream partner spell

TOOLS Several pieces of paper | Pen (preferably red ink) | Cauldron | Lighter or matches | Your favourite lipstick or lip balm **INGREDIENTS** 1 tsp dried red or pink rose petals or dried rose buds | ½ tsp cinnamon | 1 bay leaf

This is a powerful yet simple love spell to manifest your dream partner. It is important to be very specific in this spell, as otherwise you might be sent a stray cat! Don't worry about "having high expectations" or being "too demanding" - you deserve someone who makes you truly happy.

For this spell it's a good idea to cast a circle of protection. Cleanse yourself, your space, your tools and ingredients, and ground and centre yourself (see pages 26-27). Now take your pen and paper and write a list of what you seek in a partner. Describe them in great detail and while doing so, try to visualize all these details - making the image in your mind come to life. Once your list is complete, fold it three times towards yourself, rotating the paper clockwise to bring the energy you are creating towards you.

Apply the lip balm or lipstick onto your lips and kiss the folded paper. Toss it into your cauldron. Now add the dried flowers, cinnamon, and the bay leaf to the cauldron and burn them. While the flames carry your wishes onto the winds and out into the world, visualize your own happiness and love that you will experience in this relationship. Speak the words:

May the fire set my wishes free,
to bring forth divine love to me,
so mote it be.

Then open your circle, collect the ashes, and go out into nature. Face the direction of fire (see page 182) and blow the ashes to the wind. Speak the words:

May the wind set my wishes free,
to bring forth divine love to me,
so mote it be.

BEST TIME Waxing Moon, Fridays around the Spring Equinox (though can be performed any time of the year)

Are they right for me? divination

TOOLS Carving tool | 1 red or pink candle | Fireproof container or plate | Lighter or matches **INGREDIENTS** 1 fresh rose

This spell is an adaptation of the traditional folk practice of picking the petals from a flower, saying or singing "They love me, they love me not". It can help in determining if your love interest is the right person for you.

Carve the name of your love interest into the candle. Stick the candle to the plate or container. Pick the rose petals, placing them in a love heart shape around the candle, while speaking the words:

Are they right for me, are they not?

Light your candle and focus on the flame. Try to identify any symbols or shapes. If the candle flame goes out by itself, it is a definite "no". If the flame is steady and tall, the answer is "yes". If the flame flickers or is struggling to maintain height, it may indicate possible issues in the relationship. Once the candle has fully burned, look for any shapes in the candle wax that may indicate your answer.

BEST TIME Monday, New Moon

Enchanted necklace

TOOLS Necklace

This enchanted necklace spell is inspired by a folktale of a magickal seductive necklace. Wear the necklace when you wish to be especially alluring, on dates, or simply when you go out and wish to make a romantic connection.

Start by rubbing your hands together until they are warm and tingly. Now take your necklace between your hands as if in prayer. Start raising energy by focusing on your heartbeat and breathing; you can hum or flex

your hands too. Feel the necklace warming up with your energy and say the words:

I bless and consecrate this necklace, may you be enchanted for the purpose of calling romantic love to me, may I be especially alluring and charming when wearing, so mote it be.

To activate the spell, simply wear the necklace.

BEST TIME New Moon or Full Moon

LOVE AND SEX

Lover come to me candle

TOOLS Mortar and pestle | Fireproof plate | 1 red or pink chime candle (can also be a human figure candle) | Lighter or matches | Spoon | Wet-wipes (this spell gets sticky) **INGREDIENTS** 1 tsp coffee | 1 tsp dried red rose petals | 1 tsp dried honeysuckle | Maple syrup (enough to coat your candle)

This spell is intended to bring a romantic relationship into your life. Although you can personalize this so it is specific to a certain person, be mindful of possible outcomes.

Start by casting a circle and grounding and centring, and cleansing your altar space and the tools (see pages 26-27). Grind together the coffee, the rose petals, and the honeysuckle in a clockwise motion until they are a fine powder. Then set up the plate on your altar. Using the maple syrup, create a spiral going down the candle. Use the spoon to cover the candle in the ground herbs - they should stick to the syrup-covered candle easily.

Now stick the candle to the plate and wipe your hands. Light your candle and say the words:

As I light this candle, I open myself to divine, healthy, romantic love, filled with happiness and support. May this candle be a beacon in the dark to the person that is right for me, so we may find each other quickly. So mote it be.

Visualize romantic love coming to you while the candle is burning out. Then open the circle, collect the remaining wax, and bury it.

BEST TIME Friday, New Moon, Waxing Moon, Full Moon

A lovely sigil

INGREDIENTS Romantic love oil (see page 99) or rose or coconut oil

To quickly attract love to you, draw this sigil onto your skin each morning. This can also be done before being intimate to enhance your experience.

Start by creating a sigil of love (see page 22). Use the sentence "I draw love to me" or words of your choosing. While creating your sigil, visualize your intent. You can incorporate common symbols such as love hearts into your sigil. With your love oil (or rose or coconut oil) draw the sigil on your skin, or on your partner's skin, whenever you wish to draw extra romance and love into your life.

BEST TIME Friday, Waxing Moon

Broken heart bath ritual

TOOLS Bathtub | 1 black tea light candle | 1 white tea light candle | Lighter or matches
INGREDIENTS 270g (9½oz) salt (Epsom or table salt) | 1 handful lemon balm | 1 tsp cinnamon
| 3 white roses | 1 tsp lavender

This bath uses the powers of herbs and flowers, as well as the cleansing properties of water – and the symbolism of draining the water – to assist in healing and releasing the pain of a broken heart.

Draw your bath and light the tea light candles. Now add the salt, lemon balm, cinnamon, roses, and lavender to your bathtub, while being mindful of your intentions. Sink into the bathwater and let the infused water soak into your skin. Visualize the water as well as the ingredients cleansing you from pain, healing your heart. Let go of any leftover sorrows. This is also a great time to let any lingering emotions out – if you want to cry or scream, do so. The water will absorb your pain, cleanse you, and wash it away. Sit for a while, and take a moment to simply focus on your breathing and the beating of your heart. You can say your own words or:

Let my sorrows wash away, may my heart be healed of pain, may the water clean away what has left me in such bane. So mote it be.

Use the ingredients in the bath like a sponge, lightly rubbing down your entire body with them, so they can truly soak up your pain. When the water cools, get out of the bath and drain the water, visualizing all the heartbreak flowing away to be neutralized by nature.

Collect the herbs, wash them so no salt is left on them, and either take them to a river or the ocean to be released, or discard them in a bin.

BEST TIME Waning Moon

Goodbye sock spell

TOOLS New pair of socks | Thread and needle (the thread should be the same colour as the socks)

This spell is based on the Latvian superstition that to gift a sock to a lover is a sure way to have them leave you, as the sock gives them the means to walk away. It can be used when you wish to break up with your partner, but perhaps don't know how to, or it can even encourage them to initiate the break-up. Your partner doesn't necessarily have to wear the socks – the act of simply gifting the socks carries enough symbolism.

Start by casting a circle and grounding and centring, and cleansing your altar space and the tools (see pages 26-27). Take your socks and pick a spot where you can easily sew a small rune or your own sigil. With your thread and needle, sew in your sigil (see page 22) or the rune Raido, the rune of ends and journeys (see page 21). Be sure to make the rune or sigil as small and inconspicuous as possible, so it may go unnoticed. While sewing, speak the words:

May we part, and walk our separate ways, I cut these ties of heart, let this mark the end of our relationship's days. So mote it be.

Once you have sewn one sock, repeat the same for the second sock, and hold the pair in your hands, focusing on your intention and filling the socks with that energy. Envision exactly how you imagine your partner walking away, perhaps with them having initiated the break-up. Be mindful of the emotions you are feeling and focus on how you would like things to end. Adding anger or more baneful emotions may require extra protective work (see pages 40-45).

Ground and centre to finish this spell and open the circle. The pair of socks is now ready to be gifted to your partner.

BEST TIME Saturday

Letting go of the ex ritual

TOOLS Small black candle | Lighter or matches | Picture of your ex-partner | Pen | Cauldron | A box | All gifted items from the ex-partner **INGREDIENTS** A sprinkle of salt

This ritual can be done multiple times if needed, and will assist in letting go of an ex-partner.

Start by casting a circle and grounding and centring, then cleansing your altar space and the tools (see pages 26-27). Light your candle and on the picture write the incantation:

Thank you for your valuable lessons, I now release you from my life for good, so mote it be.

Then light the picture with the candle flame, and toss it in the cauldron so you don't burn yourself. Sprinkle with salt – to fully cleanse yourself of the person and let go for good – and watch the picture burn. Blow out the candle with purpose. Then toss the candle and ashes in a bin. Open the circle.

The morning after the spell, gather anything that was gifted to you, or that reminds you of your ex-partner, in a box and cleanse each item (see page 27). Donate the box to charity or throw away items that cannot be donated.

BEST TIME Waning Moon, Midnight

Break-up cord-cutting spell

TOOLS Two black candles (chime or human-shaped resembling you and your (ex-)partner) | Needle, thorn, or toothpick | Cord (natural or black) | Fireproof plate | Lighter or matches | Scissors (optional)

When a relationship is over, sometimes emotional ties can still persist. Maybe one partner is not ready to fully let go, and the entire situation simply needs to be brought to an end.

Start by casting a circle and grounding and centring, then cleansing your altar space and the tools (see pages 26-27). On one candle, carve your name, on the other the name of your (ex-) partner. Now take one end of the cord and tie it around the middle of one candle with a knot. Then do the same with the other candle so they are connected by the cord. Attach the candles to the fireproof plate by lightly burning the bottom of the candles

so they stick more easily. Now light both candles and watch them burn. The flames should eventually burn through the cord.

As you watch the candles burn down, notice which candle seems to burn faster or slower, and note any similarities between your situation and that of the two candles - which party seems not to want to let go, whose flames burn higher or barely at all, indicating strong or weak emotions in the relationship.

How fast or how slowly the candle and cord burn can also be indicative of how long the final ties in the relationship will take to break. Let the candles burn down completely, until the cord also has burned away. However, if the ties are truly persistent, take the scissors and cut the cord. Say the incantation:

The ties are cut, this is complete, we walk our separate paths, so mote it be.

Visualize the end of the relationship, knowing that any last lingering ties are now fully cut. Then open the circle and throw away the remaining wax in the bin.

———————

BEST TIME Waning Moon

FRIENDSHIP *and* FAMILY

SPELLS

From creating a peaceful home and mending relationships,
to finding new friendships, magick can be used in all
aspects of life. The home and hearth and personal
relationships are often overlooked in spellcraft,
yet these are important matters to work with.

117 HARMONIOUS HOME

122 ANIMAL FAMILY

124 BEYOND THE VEIL

126 ENHANCED COMMUNICATION

132 MAKING FRIENDS

Harmony honey cakes

TOOLS Muffin tray | Paper muffin cases | 2 mixing bowls | Wooden spoon **INGREDIENTS** 100g (3½oz) butter | 3 tbsp honey | 200g (7oz) sugar | 2 eggs | 1 tsp vanilla extract | 160ml (5½fl oz) lavender milk (see tip) | 120ml (4½fl oz) lemon juice | 270g (9½oz) plain flour | 2 tsp baking powder | ½ tsp salt | Icing sugar for dusting

Honey, lavender, and lemon are three magickal uplifting ingredients, with the power to bring harmony and happiness to the table.

Preheat the oven to 180°C (160°C fan/350°F/ Gas 4), and prep the muffin tray with paper muffin cases. Draw sigils of harmony (see page 22) on the underside of the muffin cases for extra power. In a mixing bowl, combine and cream the butter, honey, and sugar, then add in the eggs, vanilla, lavender milk, and lemon juice. In a separate bowl, sift together the flour, baking powder, and salt, then slowly fold together with the wet ingredients. As you mix, set your intentions and say the words:

As I mix, let the magick combine,
harmony and happiness come
to our family, so mote it be.

Pour the mixture into the muffin trays and bake for 30 minutes or until an inserted toothpick comes out clean. Dust with icing sugar.

BEST TIME Saturday, Full Moon
TIP To make the lavender milk, infuse the milk with a handful of fresh lavender flowers on the hob. Do not boil, just warm up and let it infuse for 1 hour (or overnight in the fridge for extra lavender flavour). Then strain so you are left with just the milk.

Happy home floor wash

TOOLS Knife | Bucket | Mop **INGREDIENTS** 1 whole fresh lemon | 3 drops vanilla oil | 3 drops hyacinth oil | 1 litre (1¾ pints) clean water

This floor wash is an easy way to cleanse your family home, bringing more harmony and the joyful feeling of sunshine.

Start by cutting the lemon into thin slices. Add the lemon and the essential oils to the bucket along with the clean water. Let the ingredients infuse the water for 10 minutes then mop your floor as usual. With each swish of the mop, visualize any negative energy being wiped away and a sheen of peachy yellow colours, which uplift the mood and bring happiness to the household, replacing it. Say the incantation:

May all negative and stagnant energies
be washed away, and left instead happiness
and blissfulness. So mote it be.

BEST TIME Friday or Waxing Moon

Family garden ritual

TOOLS Plant pots for each member | Soil | Seeds (easy plants to grow include lettuce, potatoes, or cacti) | Shovel | Marker **INGREDIENTS** Full Moon water (see tip page 34)

This ritual is intended to protect and nourish happiness and good fortune within your family or household.

Start by cleansing your ingredients by rubbing your hands together until warm, then holding them over the ingredients and saying:

May these ingredients be cleansed and blessed.

Take the pots, representing a family or household member, and bury a few of the seeds in each one. Label each pot with the name of the person. It is highly recommended to talk to the seeds to infuse them with some of your energies. Water with some of the Full Moon water. Speak the words:

I sow you with pure intentions, of love and happiness, protection and peace, may you grow strong and steady, so mote it be.

These plants will be defenders for each family member – the name ties them to that person – so take good care of them. Be sure to also check how each of the plants are doing – if one unexpectedly seems to have something wrong with it, check on that family member and ask if they are okay. Water regularly with Full Moon water, and you could also place protective crystals (see pages 180–181) around them.

BEST TIME Full Moon

Peaceful hearth pie

TOOLS Rolling pin | Pie dish | Toothpick | Bowl **INGREDIENTS** 450g (1lb) shortcrust pastry (chill in the fridge first) | 950g (2lb 2oz) blueberries (fresh or frozen) | 5 tbsp cornflour | 200g (7oz) sugar | 1 tsp salt | 1 tsp cinnamon | 1 tsp vanilla extract | 1 tsp lemon juice | 1 egg

For this recipe you will combine kitchen magick with sigil magick by carving a sigil into the pie crust to call more peace to your home. This spell works especially well as peacemaker if there has been a recent argument or other negative emotions in the home.

Preheat the oven to 190°C (170°C fan/375°F/Gas 5). Roll out the chilled pastry and divide it into two. Place one half into your pie dish to form the base. With the toothpick, lightly carve your own sigil of peace (see page 22) or the rune Wunjo (see page 21) into the base. In a bowl combine the blueberries, cornflour, sugar, salt, cinnamon, vanilla extract, and lemon juice. Stir lightly and clockwise to invoke peace and say the incantation:

Whilst I stir I combine thee, the associated correspondence of each part, may peace be called forth by me, and spread from stomach to heart.
So mote it be.

Transfer the filling into the pie crust and cover with the second piece of rolled-out pastry. At this point, you could decorate your pie, add more sigils, or keep it simple by poking a few holes into the top with a fork. Beat the egg and wash over the pie, then bake for 1 hour. Let it cool and enjoy!

———————————

BEST TIME Saturday, Full Moon

A lovely living room jar spell

TOOLS Small glass jar | Incense | Small funnel | Pen or pencil | White chime candle (or hot glue gun with white glue) | Lighter or matches
INGREDIENTS ½ tsp lavender | ½ tsp vervain | ½ tsp dried sunflower petals | ½ tsp mugwort | Clear Quartz crystal chips

Jar spells draw in energy, making this the perfect type of spell to invite some positivity into your family living room. It will promote peace and happiness, while also providing protection.

Start by cleansing your glass jar with incense. Layer in the lavender, vervain, sunflower petals, mugwort, and the crystal chips. You can speak a simple affirmation into the jar:

May happiness and peace be drawn to this space, may this space be filled with love and comfort, a space of safety and protection, so mote it be.

Close the jar and seal it by dripping candle wax around the lid, or alternatively use the hot glue gun. Now place the jar somewhere in your living room or communal space that would benefit from a dose of positive energy.

BEST TIME Saturday, Waxing Moon, Full Moon

A piece of your pet talisman

TOOLS Incense | Small pouch, locket, or bottle on a chain
INGREDIENTS Taglock (a small item that reminds you of your pet – such as fur, a picture, and so on)

When a beloved pet passes away, this talisman is a way of connecting to them in spirit, keeping their energy close by, and asking their spirit to assist and protect you from beyond the veil.

Start by casting a circle and grounding and centring, and cleansing your altar space and the tools (see pages 26–27). Light the incense and say the words:

My beloved pet, I invite you here today to join me in making a blessed talisman to keep with me. Please add your essence to this memorabilia, may it keep you close to my heart. May you protect and guide me and offer comfort as you always have.
So mote it be.

Now take your pouch, locket, or bottle, carefully add the taglock, and close the container. Hold it in both hands and visualize your beloved pet by your side while you bless and consecrate this talisman. Then give your thanks, kiss the talisman, and open the circle.

––––––––––

BEST TIME Dusk, New Moon

A blessed pet bed spell

TOOLS Paper | Pen

It's just as important to protect and bless your pet's space as it is your own.

Sit by the space that you wish to bless, and ground and centre (see page 27). Focus on the energies of blessing and protecting. Take the piece of paper and pen, and write your protective sigil (see page 22) and the name of your pet/s. Hold your hands over the paper, raise your personal energy, and visualize the sigil in your mind dissolving, activating it. Say the words:

Blessed and protected be my pet/s, may this space be a place of safety and comfort, so mote it be.

Hide the paper near your pet's space, somewhere safe so they do not try to eat it.

––––––––––

BEST TIME Monday, Saturday, Sunday, New Moon, Full Moon

Connecting to ancestors ritual

TOOLS Table, shelf, or box to use as altar | Pictures, jewellery, anything you may have that belonged to your ancestor | Glass of water (or specific drink or food if you know what they liked) | Any other tokens that feel right | Pen | Paper | 1 white or black votive candle | Lighter or matches | Cauldron

For this ritual, you will first create an ancestor altar, which will become a special place to connect you to your ancestors.

First, cleanse the new space, and set up your ancestor altar in the same way you'd set up your regular altar (see pages 20-23). Start the ritual by casting a circle and grounding and centring (see pages 26-27), and inviting your ancestors to the ritual. Next, take the piece of paper and pen and write a letter, either introducing yourself or greeting your ancestors as you would an old friend. State your intention – to connect and build a relationship – and tell them about yourself, or write about times that your ancestor has not been able to share with you. Then, fold the letter, light your candle, and burn the letter to release the message into the air. Say the words:

May this message reach you swiftly and surely, so mote it be.

Thank and release the spirits, and open the circle. Watch for signs to come, such as animals or insects that you may have never seen in your area before, or sudden random smells with no source. An additional step you can take is to ask for messages from your ancestors using tarot cards or other divinatory tools – note these in your journal.

BEST TIME Dusk or dawn, New Moon

Farewell ritual

TOOLS Bowl | Sand or soil | Knife | 1 pomegranate | Pen | Paper or picture of person or pet who has passed away | Red or black thread | 1 black candle | Lighter or matches

This ritual is for when you wish to say your goodbyes to a passed loved one. A pomegranate is used here, a symbol of the Greek goddess Persephone.

Start by casting a circle and grounding and centring as well as cleansing the tools (see pages 26–27). Fill the bowl with the sand or soil, and draw a pentagram with your finger for protection. Next, cut your pomegranate in half but not fully, so it is still connected. Put it aside and pick up your paper or picture, and on it write the words:

Farewell dear [name], may you pass into the next stage with ease, know you are loved and thought of. May you be in peace, and may your soul find rest, so mote it be.

Or feel free to write intuitively chosen words. Then place the paper or picture inside the pomegranate and close it. Tie the thread around it securely, then light the candle and seal the pomegranate with the wax drippings. Place it in the soil or sand bowl and say your own goodbyes.

Sit in meditation, and open your senses to anything you may receive from the passed loved one, such as images in your mind, or smells and possibly even sounds, or simply a sense of presence. Take this moment to fully let go and be emotional if you feel you need to. When you sense that you have completed your goodbyes, ground and centre once more.

Then open the circle. Keep the pomegranate for three days and either bury it or dispose of it respectfully in the bin.

BEST TIME Saturday, Waning Moon

Seeing the truth

TOOLS White tea light candle | Lighter or matches | Bowl of cold water

Sometimes you may wonder what the truth was in an argument or even just a mundane situation, and you feel the need to see clearly. This spell is excellent for that.

Start by casting a circle and grounding and centring as well as cleansing the tools (see pages 26-27). Light the tea light candle and sit in meditation, focusing on the situation that you would like to see more clearly and learn the truth from. When the tea light candle has completely melted, take your bowl of water and pour the wax directly into the water, holding it a little way above the surface, while saying the words:

By water and flame, clear away all doubt and fog, let me see the truth, let me see clearly and honestly, so mote it be.

Look at the wax in the water and identify any shapes or symbols that could help you understand the situation more clearly. A good tip to identifying symbols is to refer to a dream book – though the best guide is your intuition.

BEST TIME New Moon, Full Moon

Patience crystal meditation

TOOLS Clear Quartz crystal

This is a simple ritual to invoke more patience.

Take a Clear Quartz crystal into both hands. Close your eyes, and ground and centre (see page 27), visualizing an energy circuit between you and the crystal, calming you. Say the words:

Clear Quartz may you lend me patience and fortitude, so mote it be.

BEST TIME Whenever needed

Resolving a fight candle spell

TOOLS 2 black chime candles | Large fireproof dish | Lighter or matches
INGREDIENTS Olive oil | 1 tbsp dried lavender | Handful of salt

This spell is intended to assist in resolving an argument and making amends. Of course, mundane action will likely still be required, yet this spell will greatly help in creating the necessary playing field to come together again in harmony.

Start by casting a circle and grounding and centring as well as cleansing the tools (see pages 26–27). Place the two candles on the dish at least 10cm (4in) apart from each other. Drizzle the olive oil in one large circle to encompass both candles, and sprinkle the lavender and salt in the same circle. Now light your candles. Say the words:

As we stand, a distance is between us, may it be no more, may we find each other in peace and harmony once more, so mote it be.

Slowly move both of the candles together, just a little way, until you feel some form of energetic resistance. Stop moving them, and sit in meditation, focusing on your intent of harmony. Once you feel the energy has eased off, move the candles a little closer together again, until you feel some resistance. Repeat until the candles are standing right next to each other. Speak the incantation again and then wait for the candles to burn out fully. Open the circle.

BEST TIME Wednesday, New Moon, Waxing Moon

Better communication

TOOLS Mortar and pestle | Small jar | Funnel | Charcoal disc | Lighter or matches | Cauldron **INGREDIENTS** 1 tsp dried blackberry leaves | 1 tsp dried camomile | 1 tsp dried daisies | 1 tsp dried marigold | 1 tsp dried lavender

This spell will help unblock communication and in the long-term create more understanding between you and someone in your family, household, or circle of friends.

Start by cleansing your ingredients by rubbing your hands together until warm, then holding them over the ingredients and saying:

> *May these ingredients be cleansed and blessed.*

Using the mortar and pestle, grind together the blackberry leaves, camomile, daisies, marigold, and lavender until well combined. Transfer your herbs to the jar using the funnel and say the words:

> *I bless you and charge you with the intent of communication; assist in opening doors, creating a peaceful environment, an open mind to listen, and for judgment to be burned away. So mote it be.*

Sprinkle some of the herb mix onto a lit charcoal disc inside your cauldron, releasing the fumes. With fire you burn away any blockages and the communication will travel by smoke and air.

––––––––––

BEST TIME Wednesday, Waxing Moon

Contact me spell

INGREDIENTS 1 maple leaf

This spell is to help open a door to someone that you wish to speak to again – especially after an argument or if the connection was lost with time. You should cast this spell in combination with mundane efforts of contact.

Go for a walk in nature, thinking about the person you wish to establish contact with. Focus on your intentions and find a maple leaf. Take the leaf and visualize a door and you opening it. Behind the door is the person you wish to connect with. Open the door and greet them happily. Open your eyes and blow away the maple leaf.

––––––––––

BEST TIME Waxing Moon

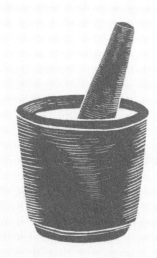

Mirror spell for self-reflection

TOOLS Mirror | Tea light candle | Lighter or matches | Small bowl

INGREDIENTS 3 drops vinegar | Sprinkle of salt

Sometimes you need to reflect on your own actions and analyse if perhaps something has been said or done that needs an apology.

Start by casting a circle and grounding and centring as well as cleansing the tools (see pages 26–27). On your altar, place the mirror so you face your own reflection, and light the candle next to the mirror. Take the bowl, add the vinegar and the salt, and with your finger stir it around clockwise, to call upon self-reflection. With the vinegar and salt mixture, draw the rune Isa in combination with Eihwaz – as Isa is a single line, draw that first, saying the rune out loud, then draw Eihwaz on top also saying it aloud (see page 21).

Next, focus on your intention of self-reflection, while looking at yourself in the mirror. At this point, allow yourself to recount the instance that you are reflecting over. Let yourself ponder and truly feel everything that comes up when thinking about it. When you feel ready, blow out the candle with intent to represent your energy mixing with that of the smoke and rising to the universe. Then open the circle.

————————————

BEST TIME Monday, Friday, New Moon

Calling a new friend crystal grid

TOOLS Agate | Blue Lace Agate | Moonstone | Clear Quartz | Rhodochrosite | Rose Quartz (or crystal chips or tumbles associated with friendship, see correspondences on pages 180–181) | Any extra tokens of your choosing

To call a new friend into your life, set up this crystal grid, which is intended to draw in opportunities that will lead to meeting new people and finding a true friend. Of course, no spell will make a friend for you - that part is still up to you.

Start by cleansing your crystals (see page 27). Pick a spot where this grid can stay for at least a week, such as a special tray on a windowsill or a shelf, as having crystals in direct sunlight for too long can damage them. Begin your grid by positioning three crystals in the shape of an upward triangle - this shape is often used as a "spirit trap", but in this case is a window to call in a friend. You can use more crystals to expand on the triangle and add extra elements such as dried flowers or shells. Consider also incorporating strings or pictures into your grid, along with any tokens that may remind you of specific traits that you are looking for in a

friend. Simply be creative and try to let your intuition guide you. Speak intuitively about all you are looking for in a friendship, or say the words:

I call into my life a true friend to join me in adventures, happy times, and to share with them loyalty, truth, and trust, to console when needed and to uplift one another, so mote it be.

Then sit in meditation, and visualize yourself with a friend, how you may meet them, how you might become friends, and the adventures or peaceful moments you could spend together. Try to put yourself in these future moments, to truly feel them. You can repeat this meditation as often as you like, or until you've found a new friend.

BEST TIME Sunday, Waxing Moon

Friends bracelet knot spell

TOOLS 3 lengths of thread, arm's length, for each friend (pick colours intuitively) | Tokens such as bells, charms, crystal beads, or even taglocks (see tip page 30)

Weaving a bracelet to represent a friendship is one of those spells that many people perform without realizing it is a spell. Here you are intentionally weaving protection, love, and happiness into bracelets.

Sit together with your chosen friends in a circle, and start by holding hands and feeling the energy pass between you. When ready, take your own threads and pass them to your friend (if there are more than two of you, pass them along clockwise). They will make your bracelet and you will make theirs. Weave the positive intentions, luck, happiness, and protection you wish for them into the bracelet. Add any tokens you wish, and then tie it together around the wrist or ankle of your friend. When you've made all the bracelets hold hands once more and say the words:

As friends we are connected, in mind as in soul, may we always be there for one another, so mote it be.

BEST TIME Sunday, Full Moon

JOY *and*
SERENITY

SPELLS

People often gravitate towards magick when in dire need or
looking for grand spells, but a lot of magick can be more
mundane, such as creating a magickal morning routine
or carving out peace in a hectic life.

135 SUMMONING SERENITY

138 CULTIVATING CONTENTMENT

144 DREAMWORLD

148 EMOTIONAL WELLBEING

152 SEASONAL CELEBRATIONS

Balance oil

TOOLS Dropper bottle or roll-on bottle | Funnel
INGREDIENTS 10 drops sandalwood oil | 5 drops myrrh oil
| 5 drops bergamot oil | 3 drops lavender oil | Base oil
(almond or grapeseed)

This oil is intended to bring balance, serenity, contentment, and harmony. You can use it by itself or to dress candles and it's helpful in a variety of spells and rituals.

Start by cleansing your ingredients (see page 27). Add each essential oil to the bottle, saying:

*May this oil bring harmony and balance,
so mote it be.*

Then fill the rest of your jar with the base oil. Shake the bottle to activate the ingredients' energies. Apply one drop to the index finger of your dominant hand, then rub your finger and thumb together until warm. Draw the invoking pentagram (see page 23) on the inside of your other hand, feeling the energy sink in and flow through you.

BEST TIME Dusk, Full Moon
NOTE For topical use only

Good vibes crystal grid

TOOLS Amethyst | Blue Lace Agate | Rose Quartz | Clear Quartz | Moonstone (or any crystal chips or tumbles associated with serenity and peace, see correspondences on pages 180–181) | Hot glue or superglue | A large mirror with frame

Making this crystal grid will create positive energy, as well as spreading it. It can be performed together with family members, even if they do not practise magick.

Start by cleansing your crystals and mirror (see page 27). Place the mirror in front of you and create a sun image with all your crystals, sticking each one in place when you are happy with the design. You could also add extra tokens such as dried flowers or shells to this grid. Say the words:

*May this grid spread around the room positive
energy, serenity, and peace, so mote it be.*

Hang this mirror somewhere it will reflect the positive energies around the room.

BEST TIME Friday, Saturday, Full Moon

Enchanted hot chocolate

TOOLS Favourite mug **INGREDIENTS** Cup of dairy or non-dairy milk | 3–4 tsp chocolate powder | Pinch of cinnamon | Splash of Full Moon water (see page 34) | A mint candy cane (or other mint-flavoured sweet)

Hot chocolate already brings joy by itself – to create an enchanted version, add a splash of moon water, a pinch of cinnamon, and a small amount of mint (a candy cane or other mint-flavoured sweet). Stir clockwise three times, then with your spoon draw the rune Wunjo (see page 21), rune of joy, comfort, and pleasure, saying a simple intuitive affirmation or the words:

Joy and happiness this drink brings to me, so mote it be.

Drink mindfully, thinking of moments that have brought you happiness, or future moments that would bring you happiness. Enjoy your drink by your altar.

―――――――――
BEST TIME Anytime

Morning tea spell

TOOLS Favourite mug or cup | Spoon
INGREDIENTS Tea or coffee

In the morning when you prepare your tea or coffee, use intention to create a magickal daily ritual. Stir your drink clockwise three times to draw in positive energy, then stir anticlockwise three times to banish negative energy. Visualize a light flowing from the Earth below you, the sky above you, and the energy within you passing through your hands into your drink. Enjoy by your altar.

―――――――――
BEST TIME Anytime, Mornings

Lavender bath ritual

TOOLS Bathtub | An organza pouch or bag | Tea light candles (as many as you like, lavender scented) | Lighter or matches **INGREDIENTS** 1 tsp dried lavender | 1 tsp dried camomile | 1 tsp dried sage | 3 drops lavender oil

This ritual is ideal for days when you wish to unwind and relax. It is especially good just before bedtime, as it induces sleepiness and relaxation.

Draw a nice hot bath. While the water is running, light the tea light candles and place them around the bathroom. Assemble all the ingredients and add them to the organza pouch. Tie a knot in the top and whisper onto the pouch intuitively chosen words or the incantation:

To bring peace and serenity, so mote it be.

Get into your bath when it's ready and dip your pouch into the hot water to infuse your bathwater. Let the scents and the powers of the herbs bring you serenity. Meditate and enjoy the energies of the water calming you, washing away any stress. When you are ready to get out, drain the water and as it flows away, let all your anxieties flow away with it.

BEST TIME Anytime, Friday and Saturday. Any moon phase, Full Moon is especially good.

Happiness manifestation

TOOLS Bowl of sand | Yellow chime candle | Lighter or matches | Bowl of sun water (see tip, page 49) **INGREDIENTS** 1 lemon, sliced | 1 orange, sliced | Handful of sunflower petals

This spell is intended to draw in happiness, laughter, sunshine, and all things that come to mind when you think of happy times.

Start by casting a circle and grounding and centring as well as cleansing the tools (see pages 26–27). Place your bowl of sand in the centre of your altar, and place the candle in the centre in the sand. Then, place the lemon and orange slices around the candle and sprinkle the sunflower petals in a circle around them. Light your candle and say the words:

Sunshine and happiness, bliss and merriment come my way, by earth, air, fire, and water I summon you into my life, so mote it be.

Take the bowl of water and dip your hands into it, sprinkling some of the water around the candle, taking care not to extinguish the flame. Sit in meditation, visualizing a sunny golden light floating towards you from all four cardinal directions, entering your body and warming you up. Sit until the candle has burned out, then open your circle. Collect the leftovers – you could cleanse the sand and reuse it in another spell – and bury the biodegradable items.

BEST TIME Sunday, Full Moon, New Moon

Happiness oil

TOOLS Dropper bottle or roll-on bottle | Funnel **INGREDIENTS** 5 drops apple oil | 3 drops orange oil | 3 drops jasmine oil | Base oil (almond or grapeseed) | 3 sunflower petals | A few Citrine chips

This is an uplifting oil to use on your skin, or in a variety of spells and rituals.

Start by cleansing your ingredients (see page 27). Add each oil to the bottle, while saying:

Together I bring the energy of the sun, of happiness and bliss, so mote it be.

Shake the bottle to activate the ingredients' energies, add one drop to both index fingers, and rub together with your thumbs. Now touch your fingers lightly on your temples, your throat, your heart, and your navel. Visualize a little sun at each spot, radiating happiness throughout your entire body and spreading out into the energetic field surrounding you.

———————

BEST TIME Friday, Full Moon
NOTE For topical use only

Bay leaf spell for happiness

TOOLS Pen | Cauldron | Lighter or matches **INGREDIENTS** A bay leaf

This quick spell is intended to bring happiness into your life, though you could easily adapt it to any other wish you have.

On your bay leaf, write the word "happiness", or any word synonymous with happiness, joy, or serenity. Light the bay leaf and drop it into your cauldron. Watch the fire burn the leaf until only ashes remain, visualizing the bliss you wish to manifest.

———————

BEST TIME Waxing or Full Moon

Happiness jar spell

TOOLS Small glass jar | Small funnel | A yellow or orange chime candle (alternatively hot glue gun with yellow or orange hot glue) **INGREDIENTS** 1 dried crushed bay leaf | Several cut pieces of dried lemon peel | Several cut pieces of dried orange peel | 1 geranium flower (or sunflower petals or dandelion) | Chips of crystals associated with happiness (see pages 179–180) | Oil (almond, olive, or vegetable)

Jar spells are intended to draw in energy and contain it. Having happiness in a jar is a beautiful way to hold onto joy and bring sunshine into your life.

Start by cleansing your glass jar (see page 27). Layer in the bay leaf, the lemon and orange peel, the flower or petals, and the crystal chips. Fill the jar with oil, leaving a little space for air. Now speak into the jar things that bring you happiness. Close the jar, sealing it by dripping candle wax around the lid (alternatively use the hot glue gun). Keep this jar safe, for example, on your altar. Shake every so often to activate the energies of the spell. Whenever you feel you need a boost, meditate holding the jar, feeling the positive energies flowing into you, filling you with peace and happiness.

BEST TIME Sunday, Waxing Moon or Full Moon

Happy knot braid

TOOLS 1 arm's length of yellow thread | 1 arm's length of white thread | 1 arm's length of orange thread **INGREDIENTS** Small beads, charms, or tokens to be plaited in

Inspired by traditional knot magick, this braid brings happiness and positive energy, and can incorporate any other magickal attribute you wish to integrate. It can be used as a bracelet or to adorn your hair.

Start by grounding and centring and cleansing your tools (see pages 26-27). Tie an initial knot with the three threads to start your braid and as you do so, speak the words:

I start this spell with the intent to draw happiness towards me, may it weave and spread throughout my life.

At this point, focus on your intent – listening to uplifting music could also assist in this. Start plaiting your threads, adding in any charms or beads every once in a while, if you like. As each thread overlaps, you are plaiting in and setting the intention of happiness coming your way, weaving it into your life. When the threads are fully braided, say the words:

The spell is done, a braid of happiness and sunshine I now have, I tie the braid together with this knot, so mote it be.

In the morning, place your braid in direct sunshine until the sun starts to set, so it has soaked up all the energies of the sun from the day. Tie it around your wrist, as tight as feels comfortable, weave it into your hair, or use it as a hair tie.

BEST TIME Friday, Saturday, Sunday, Waxing Moon

Flying ointment

TOOLS Large jar | Double boiler or two pans | Cheesecloth
INGREDIENTS 240ml (8fl oz) olive oil | 2 tsp mugwort, thinly grated | 2 tsp jasmine | 30g (1oz) beeswax | 3 drops sandalwood oil.

Dreams carry subconscious information, and flying ointments are used to induce astral travel and lucid dreams. Historically, they would have contained psychedelics or toxic nightshade plants. Some people used flying ointments to rub on brooms, hence the witch-flying-on-broom stereotype.

This recipe requires more time and effort than most. Pour the olive oil into a large jar and add the mugwort and jasmine. Close the lid and let this oil infuse for at least a month in a cool, dark place.

Once infused, pour the oil through the cheesecloth into the double boiler on a low heat, squeezing out the mugwort and jasmine. Add the beeswax, and slowly warm up the oil – do not overheat or bring to the boil. Once the beeswax and the oil have combined, add the sandalwood oil and stir. Transfer to the jar and let it harden.

Before going to sleep, take a pea-sized amount of the salve, rub onto your wrists, and say:

Tonight I fly, in my dreams and in spirit,
to a world of wonder, so mote it be.

BEST TIME New Moon, Full Moon
NOTE For topical use only

Remembering your dreams spell

TOOLS Mortar and pestle | Airtight container **INGREDIENTS** 1 tsp basil | Sprinkle of dried sage | 1 tsp rosemary | 1 tsp comfrey | 3 drops patchouli oil | 1 tsp water | 1 tsp honey | Lighter or matches

Our dreams can at times be prophetic or insightful, delivering messages from our subconscious. They can even be a way of processing past experiences. Tapping into and recalling dreams is another way to work with the energies and subconscious in your path. For this spell, you will make your own incense cones.

Start by cleansing your ingredients, rubbing your hands together until warm, then holding them over the ingredients, saying:

May these ingredients be cleansed and blessed.

With the mortar and pestle, grind together the dry ingredients, stirring clockwise to draw the memories of your dreams towards you. Once the herbs are fine and well combined, add the patchouli oil and mix again. Repeat with the water and lastly the honey. Using your fingers, form pyramid shapes or cones. Let these dry for 1–2 days and then store in an airtight container.

Half an hour before going to sleep, sit by your altar, and light one of your incense cones. Say this incantation three times:

Memories of dreams past, present, and future, come to me easily, so mote it be.

Perform this spell frequently throughout your week for the best results.

_____

BEST TIME Anytime

Create your own dream

TOOLS Paper | Pen | Cauldron | Lighter or matches | Small satchel or bag **INGREDIENTS** Flying ointment (page 144) or 1 tsp peppermint | Pinch of mugwort | Pinch of valerian root | 1 star anise

For this spell, you will set the intention of your dreams, so you may find yourself in that dreamworld when sleeping. This technique can also assist in working towards lucid dreaming.

Before going to sleep, take the paper and pen and write in as much detail as you can about the dreamworld you would like to visit. Visualize this as you write it out, and start imagining all you can see, feel, and hear there. When you have written as much as you can, fold the paper three times towards you, drawing in the dream, then burn it. As the smoke rises, visualize it becoming energy that will reach you in your dreams. At this point, intuitively speak an incantation or say:

I create my dreams to be immersed in a world of fantasy and adventure, so mote it be.

Then, either rub a pea-sized amount of flying ointment on your wrists, or fill a small bag or satchel with the peppermint, mugwort, valerian root, and star anise. Cleanse and bless the bag and place it under your pillow.

BEST TIME Anytime

Dream recorder crystal enchantment

TOOLS Clear Quartz and/or Amethyst

This technique is called programming, and in this specific instance it is performed to improve your dream recall.

Take a Clear Quartz or Amethyst crystal and cleanse it by smoke, sound, or your own energy (see page 27). Now hold the crystal in both hands and focus on your intent – to remember your dreams and "record" them using this crystal. Visualize a video recorder inside of it, and say the words:

I program you to record my dreams, may I be able to tap into and clearly recall them, so mote it be.

Place this crystal under your pillow or next to your bed, and tap your crystal before going to sleep, saying "start recording". In the morning, tap the crystal again and say, "stop recording".

Meditate with your crystal in your hands to remember your dreams. With time and practice, recalling your dreams will become easier and your memories more vivid.

BEST TIME Anytime, Full Moon

Peaceful sleep charm bag

TOOLS Cotton or linen pouch or piece of cloth | Dark blue thread Needle | Dark blue marker **INGREDIENTS** 1 tsp lavender | 1 tsp marjoram | 1 violet | 1 star anise | 1 Amethyst crystal

This charm bag is intended to help you have more restful and peaceful sleep, free of nightmares, and is to be placed in or under your bed. Frequently cleanse the bag to release energy and recharge it.

Start by casting a circle, grounding and centring, and cleansing your altar space and tools (see pages 26-27). Take your piece of cloth or pouch and using either the thread and needle, or the marker, sew or draw on a sigil of good sleep, or the rune Laguz (see pages 21-22). Before tying the pouch to close it, say the words:

Good sleep and rest come to me, banish all nightmares and sleepless nights, so mote it be.

Now tie together your charm bag with the thread. Ground and centre and open the circle.

Place your bag under your pillow or near your bed. Before going to sleep, visualize a pulsating shield of energy growing out of the pouch, encompassing you and your bed as well as any partner, children, or pets. Fall asleep knowing you have a shield of protection around you.

BEST TIME Full Moon, New Moon

Anti-anxiety spell jar

TOOLS Incense to cleanse | Lighter or matches | Small glass jar | Small funnel | Purple chime candle (alternatively hot glue gun with purple hot glue) | Pen **INGREDIENTS** 1 tsp dried lavender | 1 tsp dried camomile | 1 tsp dried jasmine | 1 Blue Lace Agate crystal | 1 bay leaf

This spell jar is perfect to assist with managing anxiety, though of course this does not replace professional attention. Keep it near you in a bag, or next to your bed. Spell jars contain and radiate energy - this one is intended to dissipate the anxious energy within and around you, and spread calming energy.

Start by cleansing your glass jar with incense - lavender is a good choice. Layer in the dried lavender, camomile, jasmine, and the Blue Lace Agate crystal. Now write the word "serenity" on your bay leaf and add it to the jar. Close the jar, sealing it by dripping candle wax around the lid (or use the hot glue gun).

Keep this jar safe, for example on your altar. Shake every so often to activate its energies, and meditate holding it, each time feeling the anxiety easing, filling you with peace.

BEST TIME Waning Moon

Blues-banishing ritual

TOOLS A bucket of water | 2 pieces of white natural felt or cotton (about 10 x 10cm/4 x 4in) | Marker | Thread and needle | Scissors | Funnel | Mortar and pestle | Cauldron | Lighter or matches **INGREDIENTS** 1 tsp salt | 1 tsp eggshells | 1 tsp dried lavender | 1 tsp dried rosemary

This spell is intended for when you feel low. For this spell you will make a doll – a tool that has been used in various cultures throughout history. It is a form of sympathetic magick, and, as with all magick, can be whatever the practitioner makes of it.

Start by casting a circle, grounding and centring, and cleansing your altar space and tools (see pages 26–27). Set the water next to your altar, as a fire safety precaution.

Take and align the felt pieces, draw an approximate human shape, and cut it out. Ensure you draw it roughly 1cm (½in) bigger than you want the doll to be to allow space for the stitching. Take the thread and needle and make your first stitch. Focus on the intention of uplifting your emotions, and banishing the negative. Stitch around 80 per cent of the doll to leave an opening for stuffing with the herbs.

With the mortar and pestle, grind together the salt, eggshells, lavender, and rosemary. Fill the doll with the mix and sew shut, saying:

I banish all negative, depressive thoughts
and memories, I banish maleficent energies
surrounding me.
May I feel the release of these,
may positive energy come to me,
and help me on my healing journey,
so mote it be.

Now take the doll you have made and burn it in your cauldron. Visualize any negative or depressive thoughts leaving the doll and subsequently leaving you. As the herbs burn, positive energy is released surrounding you. When finished, open the circle, and throw the ashes of the doll to the wind for a final release.

_____

BEST TIME New Moon

Mental clarity charm bag

TOOLS Cotton or linen pouch or piece of cloth | White thread **INGREDIENTS** 1 walnut | 1 tsp basil | 1 tsp peppermint | 1 tsp rue | 1 Clear Quartz crystal | A feather

When in need of mental clarity, make this charm bag and use it until your thoughts and emotions have cleared.

Start by casting a circle and grounding and centring, and cleansing your altar space and the tools (see pages 26-27). Take your piece of cloth or your pouch and add all the ingredients. Loosely tie the pouch or cloth together with the white thread, but not yet fully, and say this incantation into the small opening of the pouch or cloth:

May this pouch enhance my mental and emotional clarity, to judge wisely and logically, to feel intuitively, free from influences, so mote it be.

Now fully tie together your charm bag. Ground and centre to finish this spell and open the circle.

Keep the charm bag either on your person, or place it underneath your pillow. Hold your bag every day for a week, or whenever desired. Calm your breathing, focusing on the pouch in your hands. Visualize a soothing light pulsing within the bag and slowly spreading outwards to dissipate the fog of jumbled thoughts and offer a clear perspective on your given situation. Once you feel ready, you can tuck away your charm bag for later use.

BEST TIME Full Moon, New Moon, or Waxing Moon

First harvest – bread baking ritual

TOOLS Loaf tin I Mixing bowl I Baking paper I Toothpick
INGREDIENTS 400ml (14fl oz) luke-warm water I 1 pack dry yeast I ½ tsp sugar I 450g (16oz) wholemeal flour I 2 tsp salt I 100g (3½oz) sunflower seeds I Raisins or herbs with magickal correspondence (see pages 181–183), optional

Lammas or Lughnasadh is a Gaelic festival celebrating the first harvest of the year (celebrated on 1 August in the northern hemisphere and 1 February in the south). It is traditional to honour this day by baking bread. This recipe, can be easily adjusted by adding raisins, berries, or herbs relating to a specific correspondence you'd like to invoke.

Dissolve the yeast with the sugar in the water, then mix together all the remaining ingredients, until the dough is well combined and sticky. Prepare your tin by lining it with baking paper. Transfer the dough to your tin and let it sit for 30 minutes to rise. Using the toothpick, draw sigils or runes into your dough (see pages 21–22). Alternatively, press the sunflower seeds into the top of the dough in a pattern (such as a sigil or rune). Hold your hands over your mixture and say:

For this harvest I give my thanks, may this bread bring in good health, prosperity, and fortune, so we may stay warm when winter knocks on our door. So mote it be.

Place the dough into your still-cold oven and turn it on to 240°C (220°C fan/460°F/Gas 9) for an hour.

BEST TIME Morning of first harvest

Summer solstice – flower crown ritual

INGREDIENTS A basketful of flowers (in correspondence to your intention, see pages 181–183) I A basketful of oak leaves

During the summer solstice it can be customary to wear a flower crown or a crown of leaves. This ritual is inspired by the Baltic midsummer tradition.

On the day of the summer solstice, craft yourself a flower crown by picking seasonal, local flowers. Choose them according to what you wish to bring into your life for the year to come (see correspondences, pages 182-185).

A wreath of oak leaves and branches is customary if you do not want to wear a flower crown. Flower crowns are seen as more feminine, oak leaf wreaths as masculine – pick whichever you are more comfortable with, or mix them together.

Wear your crown with pride for the entire day, especially if you are celebrating with a bonfire and friends or family later in the day. This is a time to celebrate.

Keep this wreath for the whole year, to be thrown and burned in a bonfire on midsummer a year later.

BEST TIME Morning of summer solstice

Autumn equinox – healing pumpkin soup

TOOLS Large saucepan | Knife | Chopping board | Hand-mixer or blender **INGREDIENTS** 1 pumpkin (Hokkaido is preferred as the skin is edible) | 3 medium carrots | 1 large potato | 1 onion | 500ml (16fl oz) vegetable stock | 400ml (14fl oz) coconut milk | 1cm (⅓in) fresh ginger, chopped | Salt and pepper to taste

This pumpkin soup is perfect to honour the second harvest festival and the autumn equinox.

Peel and chop the pumpkin, carrots, potato, and onion. Place them in a pan of lightly salted water and cook until soft (approximately 40 minutes to an hour). Using the lid, drain the water. Add the stock and the coconut milk and blend until combined. Add the ginger, salt, and pepper to taste, and enjoy!

BEST TIME Evening of autumn equinox

All Hallows Eve – silent supper ritual

INGREDIENTS A dish your passed loved one or ancestor would enjoy

All Hallows Eve, also known as Samhain or Day of the Dead, takes place on 31 October and marks the last of the harvest festivals. It is known as the day when the veil between our world and the spirit world is the thinnest, making it an ideal time for spirit and ancestor workings.

A traditional ritual is the silent supper. In the evening, when preparing dinner, cleanse the dinner table and make an extra dish for a passed loved one, a spirit or ancestor, or even a deity that you work with. It is customary to sit in silence for this meal to honour the dead. Serve a plate of the meal as you would for a living person. When finished, say your thanks and take the plate of food and either store it for the next day, or, if it feels more comfortable, discard it.

BEST TIME Evening of All Hallows Eve

Winter solstice – blessed yule log ritual

TOOLS Wooden log | 3 or 4 tea light candles | Winter decor (pine cones, moss, dried fruit, and so on) | Hot glue gun | Lighter or matches

The winter solstice, also known as yule or jul, is the rebirth of the sun and a time to honour winter. A tradition is to bring a yule log into your home to burn and bring in warmth.

On the winter solstice, craft a yule log using a wooden log found outside, and decorate it with the tea light candles using the hot glue gun to secure them, as well as any other winter decor you may find depending on your region.

Bless the log and light the candles on the eve. Traditionally, you would leave the fire burning all night, so using votive candles may be a safer option. Alternatively, light the candles daily until they burn down, or until first spring.

BEST TIME Evening of the winter solstice, or four weeks prior to the winter solstice

First spring – fire scrying ritual

TOOLS White candle (or alternatively use a hearth fire or bonfire if accessible) | Lighter or matches

First spring, or Imbolc, begins on the evening of 1 February and is the midway point between the winter and spring equinox and a time when the sun is getting stronger and plants and animals are reawakening. To honour this day, a simple fire scrying ritual can be performed.

Light a white candle, or use a larger body of fire such as a hearth, and sit in meditation, focusing on the flame. Ask aloud:

What can I expect to come my way soon?

Try to focus on the flame, its movement, and any shapes or symbols you may see emerging. A strong and steady flame may indicate positive experiences coming your way, whereas a weaker flame may prophesize obstacles. Be sure to cleanse and ground (see page 27) before and after this ritual.

BEST TIME Evening of first spring

Spring equinox – ostara eggs spell

TOOLS Eggs | Large cooking pot | Toothpick or needle
INGREDIENTS 1 litre (1¾ pints) water | 150g (5½oz) beetroot or red onions, for red | 150g (5½oz) turmeric or camomile flowers, for yellow | 150g (5½oz) spinach or nettles, for green | 150g (5½oz) black tea, coffee, or onion peel, for brown | 150g (5½oz) blueberries, lilac berries, or red cabbage leaves, for blue and purple

The spring equinox, also known as ostara, is a Germanic festival honouring springtime, fertility, and life. It is a great time to embark on any new projects. This simple egg spell celebrates the spring equinox.

Start by collecting several fresh eggs (it's fine to use shop bought if fresh eggs aren't available to you). Next, using a toothpick or a needle, make two holes on the top and bottom of the eggs. Now blow into one end, to remove the egg white and yolk (perfect for scrambled eggs, so do not throw away).

To dye the eggs, take a pot and add the natural colouring ingredient of your choice to the water. Bring to the boil and then let sit for another 15 minutes, before removing the dyeing ingredient. Place the eggs into the pot for several hours or overnight to soak up the colour. Using colour correspondences (see page 178) in combination with the magick of eggs (which represent growing new opportunities), you can manifest your future wishes. Hang the eggs up at your altar to welcome in your wishes.

BEST TIME Morning of the spring equinox

May Day – maypole ritual

TOOLS A flat piece of wood | 1 branch (arm's length) | Hot glue gun or drill | 3 or more coloured ribbons (arm's length) | 3 tea light candles| Lighter or matches

May Day, or 1 May, also known as Beltane or Walpurgisnacht, is all about celebrating fertility, love, and sex, and is the midpoint between the spring equinox and summer solstice. Dancing around the maypole was once a tradition in several countries in Europe - and is a long-standing tradition in Germany to this day - to celebrate the first day of summer.

To craft your own maypole as an altar adornment, use a flat piece of wood as a base and a longer wooden branch to form your maypole. Using a hot glue gun, or a drill, connect the two together. Select several coloured ribbons to tie to the top of the maypole and plait them around the branch. Traditionally, colours would correspond to regions (blue and white, for example, is very popular in Bavaria), but you can pick colours corresponding to what you would like to call into your life (see correspondences on page 178). Light the tea light candles around the maypole to represent the fire, and feast by your altar.

BEST TIME May Day morning

WORK *and* AMBITION

SPELLS

Weaving magick into everyday life includes your work and hobbies, areas of life that often have room for greater ease and growth. Perhaps you'd like more confidence, or maybe you're simply looking for inspiration.

157 SUMMONING SUCCESS

164 RING IN THE CHANGES

170 SELF-IMPROVEMENT FOR SUCCESS

Success powder

TOOLS Mortar and pestle | Jar | Tea light candle | Lighter or matches **INGREDIENTS** 1 tsp dried basil | 1 tsp dried camomile | 1 tsp red clover | 1 tsp cinnamon | 1 tsp sugar

To draw success to you, create this powder to use in spells, dress candles, or sprinkle on doorways and around your workspace.

Cleanse your ingredients by rubbing your hands together until warm, then holding them over the ingredients and saying:

May these ingredients be cleansed and blessed.

With the mortar and pestle, grind together the dry ingredients until fine. Either transfer the mix to your jar, or use immediately by sprinkling some on a tea light candle, lighting the candle and speaking words intuitively or saying:

I draw towards myself success and a positive outcome in my endeavours, so mote it be.

BEST TIME Full Moon, Waxing Moon
WISDOM Dragons, mythical beings of strength and power, are related to success, and there is a plethora of stories of dragons hoarding gold, or being a source of wisdom. Working with the energy of dragons can introduce these themes into your practice.

Sun water ritual

TOOLS Mug | Spoon **INGREDIENTS** Sun water (see tip, page 49) | Your favourite tea blend or coffee | Citrine, Fire Quartz, or Carnelian crystal

Sun water is charged by the sun and is full of the energies of success, strength, radiance, and happiness.

In your tea or coffee in the morning, add a teaspoon of sun water to call in the energies of the sun, especially if you have any projects planned for the day for which you want to ensure success. Stir clockwise to draw in, and visualize the sun's energy while drinking. For an extra boost, place a sun-associated crystal next to your mug to charge your drink. Visualize a small sun inside your crystal, radiating outwards encompassing your drink until it is radiating its own sunny energy.

BEST TIME Anytime

Manifestation bath ritual

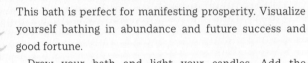

TOOLS Candles for ambience (optional) **INGREDIENTS** 700ml (1¼ pints) sun water (see tip, page 49) | 700ml (1¼ pints) milk | 3 tbsp honey | Yellow-coloured fresh flowers

This bath is perfect for manifesting prosperity. Visualize yourself bathing in abundance and future success and good fortune.

Draw your bath and light your candles. Add the ingredients to your bathwater. Climb into the bath, and visualize yourself stepping into abundance and prosperity. While soaking, continue this visualization saying:

May I bathe in abundance, happiness, and prosperity, so mote it be.

Meditate and focus on your intentions. When you feel ready, step out of the bath.

BEST TIME Sunrise, Sunday, Waxing Moon, Full Moon
TIP Feel free to use vegan substitutes like oat milk and maple syrup instead of milk and honey.

Career success shower pouch

TOOLS Small organza bag, preferably yellow or gold **INGREDIENTS** 1 tsp dried basil | 1 tsp marjoram | 1 tsp peppermint | 1 tsp cinnamon | 1 tsp thyme

Craft this pouch to hang in your shower, so every time the water cleanses you, you are also infused with the energy of motivation, ambition, happiness, and success in your career.

Cleanse your ingredients by rubbing your hands together until warm, then holding them over the ingredients and saying:

May these ingredients be cleansed and blessed.

Take the organza bag and fill it with the herbs. Close the bag and hold it in both hands, raising energy. Visualize energy from the universe above and the Earth beneath you flowing into the charm bag, charging it with golden light. Hang this in your shower and say the words:

May you shower me with success, happiness, and good fortune in my career, so mote it be.

Adjust the words if you are looking to call in a new career rather than simply find success in your current one.

_____

BEST TIME Full Moon, Waxing Moon

Ringing in customers doorbell spell

TOOLS Incense to cleanse | Pouch | Small bell | String **INGREDIENTS** 3 bay leaves | 1 tsp peppermint | 1 tsp thyme | 3 coins of your currency

Hanging a bell on the door of your work premises not only announces new customers, but cleanses and protects the space. It will also draw in more customers.

Start by cleansing your ingredients with incense. Then add the herbs and coins to the pouch and close it. Next, tie the bell to the pouch using your string, making sure it is loose enough so the bell is able to jingle when moved. Focus on your intentions while making this charm. Tie it to the front door handle, so every time someone enters, the bell rings.

_____

BEST TIME Thursday, Waxing Moon, Full Moon

Charmed clothing spell

TOOLS Thread and needle (or marker) | Piece of clothing | Small square piece of cotton (approx 3 x 3cm/1 x 1in)

Bringing magick into your busy day-to-day life can sometimes seem challenging, until you realize you can charm every aspect of it, including your clothing. This spell is perfect if you are going for a job interview, have an important meeting, or are giving a speech.

Cleanse your tools (see page 27), then take the small piece of cotton and sew or draw a sigil of success (see page 22) or the rune Jera (see page 21). Next, sew the piece of cotton into the inside of your clothing – ideally where the tags are positioned. While sewing, speak the intentions for this charmed clothing. You could speak intuitively or say:

May success come my way, along with peace and prosperity. So mote it be.

Visualize the rune or sigil glowing faintly, seeping its magick into your clothing.

BEST TIME Full Moon, New Moon, or Waxing Moon

Enchanted shoes sigil

TOOLS A pair of your shoes | Piece of paper or a bay leaf | Pen

A simple but effective way to draw in success throughout your day is to place a small piece of paper or bay leaf with a sigil of success (see page 22) or the rune Fehu or Jera (see page 21) in your shoes.

Start by cleansing your paper or bay leaf (see page 27) and draw the sigil or rune with the pen, focusing on your intention. Next, fold the paper towards you to draw in, or away from you if you wish to keep something away. If you are using a bay leaf you won't need to fold it. Now either place the paper or bay leaf on the sole of the shoe, or tuck it into the tongue of the shoe, where it will be secure for the day. You can also do this charm by drawing a rune or sigil directly on your shoes if you feel comfortable to do so. Remember to frequently redraw the sigil or rune if you draw it on the sole as it will wear off.

BEST TIME Full Moon, New Moon, or Waxing Moon

A Waxing Moon ritual

TOOLS Paper | Pen | Pot | Soil | Spade | Seeds, either corresponding to success or wealth (see correspondences pages 182–185) or yellow/orange flowers

This ritual is perfect for setting intentions for the upcoming months. Use it to call towards you success and courage to go after your dreams and wishes.

Start by grounding, centring, and cleansing your tools (see page 27). Tear the paper into small pieces, large enough to write a word on each. You can rip the paper into a specific number of manifestations you have in mind, or for example into 3, 9, or 13 pieces. Write keywords of things you wish to draw in, words such as "courage", "motivation", or more materialistic keywords such as "new opportunities", "promotion", or "fun new project". Roll each of these papers into small beads. Then take your pot and add the soil until almost full. Using your fingers, create indents in the soil and add the seeds and the paper beads and cover with soil. Visualize planting each intention, so it may grow into what you wish to manifest.

Hold your hands over the pot of soil, and raise energy by visualizing an energy circuit flowing from above, below, and through you into the pot, charging it with extra energy. Say the words:

By the Waxing Moon, I sow my intentions, may I reap my goals and wishes, so mote it be.

Be mindful when watering your plant or seed - focus on watering and nurturing your intentions so they may grow strong.

―――――――――

BEST TIME Waxing Moon

13-day candle spell

TOOLS Large orange or golden candle | Fireproof plate or dish | Lighter or matches **INGREDIENTS** Olive oil | 1 pinch of cinnamon | 1 pinch of dried thyme | 1 pinch of dried basil | 3 freshly picked clovers (four-leaf would be ideal, but hard to come by) | 1 tbsp salt

Cast this spell when you are trying to draw in success, whether that be in the form of money, a new job or a promotion, or opportunities. You can adapt this spell to draw in anything you may desire.

Start by casting a circle, grounding and centring, as well as cleansing all your ingredients (see pages 26–27). Take the candle, and tap it on your altar three times to wake it up, then roll it towards you to set the intention of drawing in success.

Add a few drops of olive oil to the candle and roll it in the cinnamon, thyme, and basil. Stand the candle on the plate, place the three clovers around the candle, and sprinkle a salt circle around them. Make sure the plate and candle are sitting on your altar relatively far away from you. Light the candle and speak of all you wish to draw towards you over the coming 13 days. You could say:

Over 13 days I raise this energy, to summon success and fortune to me. May I soon acquire what I desire.
So mote it be.

Now carefully pull the plate with the candle towards you slightly, visualizing success coming your way. Sit in meditation and, when ready, extinguish the candle and open the circle.

For the next 13 days, sit daily with the candle lit, repeat the incantation, and pull the candle a bit closer towards you each time.

BEST TIME New Moon

A charming talisman spell

TOOLS Pen | Orange or gold thread (arm's length)
INGREDIENTS 1 bay leaf | 1 round slice of dried apple – bake for several hours to dry

To appear more charming, create this glamour talisman for when you need to come across as extra charismatic. It's perfect for job interviews, applying for loans, or settling contracts.

Start by cleansing your ingredients (see page 27), and then take the pen and carefully write the word "charming" on the bay leaf, or alternatively a sigil of your own creation (see page 22). Place the bay leaf on the apple slice, and tightly wrap the thread around the apple and bay leaf. Hold the new talisman in your hands, visualizing energy flowing into it, and say:

I bless and consecrate this talisman, to create an energetic field around me of charm, so mote it be.

Now tuck away your talisman in a pocket or bag that you are likely to be wearing or have on you when in need of your charm. If this talisman has a more specific intention, such as attaining a certain job position, you can bury it once it is no longer of use, giving back to nature.

BEST TIME Thursday, Sunday, New Moon

A CV sigil

TOOLS An eraser or an editing program on your computer or phone | Pen | Paper

Create this hidden sigil to add to your CV when applying for jobs to increase your chances of landing the role. Depending on if you submit online or in person, you can adjust this spell to successfully hide the sigil in the document.

Create a sigil using a phrase such as: "I will land this job", (see page 22). Then, if you are submitting a paper copy of your CV, use the eraser to "write" the sigil on it. If you're sending a digital document, upload your sigil by taking a picture of it, adding the image to the document, and reducing the visibility to 0. When you send out your CV, visualize your sigil evaporating, activating it.

BEST TIME Thursday, Waxing Moon, Full Moon

Fast employment charm bag

TOOLS Small pouch or piece of cloth | Gold or orange thread | Needle | Piece of paper | Pen **INGREDIENTS** 1 tsp red clover | 1 tsp cinnamon | 1 tsp vervain | 1 crystal tumble, Amber or Carnelian

Create this little charm bag to help with securing employment, as both a glamour for yourself as well as for a boost in confidence. Carry it with you when you attend interviews or when you are job hunting.

Cleanse all your tools and ingredients (see page 27). Then sew a sigil of success, or the rune Dagaz (see pages 21-22), onto your pouch and add the ingredients. Take the piece of paper and write the incantation:

Opportunity come to me, may it suit me well, to make me carefree, and bring me mental and physical stability I compel. So mote it be.

Fold the paper towards you three times and add to the pouch.

Next, hold your pouch in both hands and take a moment to take a few deep breaths. Start raising energy (see page 27), letting it flow from you into the pouch, visualizing your hands and the pouch glowing faintly in gold or green (whichever colour you associate with success, see correspondences page 178). When you feel that the pouch has filled up with energy, let the light settle completely in the pouch and set aside. Ground and centre to finish.

BEST TIME New Moon, Waxing Moon, Full Moon

Finding a new job spell

TOOLS Pen | Paper | Fireproof plate or cauldron | 1 white chime candle | Needle, thorn, or toothpick | Lighter or matches

Finding a new job can be tough, and finding a job that suits your lifestyle and dreams even more so. This spell should be repeated weekly during the period of the Waxing Moon.

Start by casting a circle, grounding and centring, as well as cleansing your ingredients (see pages 26–27). Sit in meditation, focusing on the career you wish to manifest. Try to imagine yourself already having your ideal job and the emotions you would experience. On the piece of paper, write out what your ideal job position would look like. Be as specific as possible, including salary and working hours, but do stay within the realms of reality. Fold the paper once towards you, placing it under the plate. Next, take the candle and, using the needle, carve either a sigil of your own creation or the rune Gebo (see pages 22–21), then attach the candle to the plate and light it. Watch the candle burn, focusing on your intention.

Extinguish the candle when you feel ready and open the circle. As this spell is best performed multiple times, make sure to leave enough of the candle to burn it next time.

BEST TIME Thursday, Saturday, during Waxing Moon period (New Moon until Full Moon)

Sweet boss bowl spell

TOOLS Bowl | Pen | Paper | Fireproof plate | Lighter or matches **INGREDIENTS** 1 bay leaf | 1 tsp lavender | 1 tsp camomile | 1 tbsp honey | 240ml (8fl oz) dairy or non-dairy milk

This spell is perfect if you are having trouble with your boss or manager, and need to "sweeten" them up a bit. Using milk and honey has long been an ancient offering, especially in northern Europe, and honey jars can also be seen in closed practices such as Voodoo and Hoodoo. However, they are quite different from this spell in that honey is merely one of the ingredients.

Start by casting a circle, grounding and centring, then cleanse your bowl (see pages 26–27). On the piece of paper write the name of the person you would like to appeal to, as well as a suitable sigil of your own creation (see page 22). Fold it three times towards you and burn it, then add the ashes to the bowl. Then add the bay leaf, lavender, camomile, and the honey, and cover with milk until the bowl is full. Now mix together all the ingredients, stirring clockwise, and hold your bowl in both hands, raising and focusing your energy and intent, letting the bowl fill with energy until you feel it is full to the brim. Say the incantation:

May you sweeten up to me, to be open and courteous, kinder and gentler. May you be open to listening to me fully, willing to understand me and work together peacefully and efficiently, so mote it be.

When finished, open your circle. Take your bowl outside, pour out the contents onto the soil, saying:

Spirits of nature, I give to you this offering, may you assist me in creating a positive attitude with my [boss/superior]. So mote it be.

When finished, ground and centre again.

———————

BEST TIME Sunday, Waxing Moon, Full Moon

Find a new home manifestation ritual

TOOLS White tea light candle | Lighter or matches | Estate agents' brochures | A printer | Scissors | Pins or glue | Pinboard, magnetic board, large empty picture frame, or digital device to create your vision board | Mortar and pestle **INGREDIENTS** Bay leaf | 1 pinch of cinnamon | 1 eggshell

A technique you can use for manifesting is to create a vision board, enabling you to physically see the things you wish to manifest daily and get into the mindset of that reality. This can help you be open to more opportunities, or come up with new ideas that could lead you directly to your desired goals. This ritual is specifically for finding a new home.

Gather all your ingredients and cleanse them (see page 27). Then grind together the bay leaf, cinnamon, and eggshell until it is a fine powder. Next, sprinkle the powder onto the lit candle (be careful as the flames can get large – sprinkle around the candle on a plate instead if you wish to avoid that). Next, start cutting out or printing pictures that align with what you wish to manifest: the style of house, the colour, the area that it is in, the budget, experiences you want to have in this home (start a family, adopt a pet, create your dream office for your small business, curate a herb garden... whatever you desire). Arrange it all so it is visually appealing to you and then speak the words:

I manifest this dream of mine, a house to call my own, this future I untwine, with this spell I have sown, so mote it be.

Hang up your vision board, or use it as wallpaper on your electronic device.

––––––––––––––

BEST TIME Thursday, Sunday
New Moon, Waxing Moon

Sweeping away doubt ritual

TOOLS A brush or broom to sweep

Sweeping has long been used both to clean and to symbolize brushing away negative energy or thoughts. In this ritual, you will sweep away self-doubt hindering you from achieving the success you desire.

Take your broom, and start to sweep your space – be sure to sweep from east to west, following the direction of the sun. While sweeping, visualize lingering self-doubt being swept up and away from your space. Say the incantation:

I sweep and sweep away the doubt, for it may hold me back no more. So mote it be.

When you have swept all the dust into one pile, throw it away. Perform this sweeping-away ritual periodically – weekly or fortnightly is best.

BEST TIME Waning Moon, New Moon

Reaching your goals knot spell

TOOLS Cord, an arm's length (natural or colour corresponding, see page 178) | Any tokens relating to the goal you want to achieve

If you are working on something that you wish to succeed in, employ this knot spell to tie your intentions into knots, using the cord to focus on your goals.

Start by centring, grounding and casting a circle (see pages 26–27). Take the cord and tie a knot at one end. Then tie each new knot closer to you, representing your goal coming closer towards you. While tying each knot, say the incantation:

With this first knot, may I set the intent, to reach my goal of [say your goals].

With the second knot, I tie in the energy to draw to me [say your goals].

With the third knot, may it hold strong and fast, so mote it be.

In between each knot add any of the tokens you like and tie a loop at the end.

Sit with the cord, visualizing your goals becoming reality. Hang the cord above your altar or in a room that would be significant to your goal – a spot where you frequently see the cord and are reminded of your goals is most suitable.

BEST TIME Thursday, New Moon, Waxing Moon

I am worthy candle ritual

TOOLS Pan of water | 1 white candle in a tin or jar | Lighter or matches | Tongs **INGREDIENTS** Sprinkle of thyme | Sprinkle of cinnamon | Sprinkle of poppy seeds | 1 dried apple slice

Sometimes you are the only thing blocking your path to success. Use this spell when you need a reminder that you are worthy of the success you have worked so hard for, and to give yourself a boost of confidence.

Start by cleansing your ingredients (see page 27), and bring the pan of water to the boil. Place the candle in a tin or jar carefully into the boiling water, without letting any of the water spill over into the candle. Wait until the wax of the candle has fully melted and carefully, using tongs, remove the candle from the water and sprinkle on the thyme and cinnamon. Then wait until the wax has hardened a bit before adding the poppy seeds and the apple slice – that way they won't sink to the bottom of the candle

and the finished product will look more attractive. Next, intuitively speak an affirmation of self-worth or you could say the words:

With spark and flame, ignite within me my power. My might I will not tame, I will not bow, I am worth all that I create and success will be mine. Remove from my shoulders the weight of self-doubt, to recognize I am divine.

Light the candle whenever you need a self-esteem boost and sit in meditation, repeating the affirmation that you spoke to enchant the candle.

BEST TIME New Moon, Full Moon, Waxing Moon

WRITE YOUR OWN SPELLS

If you create your own spell, it will carry your energy, making it more powerful for you. You can also use any spell in this book and adapt it to make it more specific to your intention.

Spells or rituals do not need to be elaborate each time – a spell can be anything into which you invest intention and so it can be easily incorporated into your everyday life. Try to think about the mundane activities you do daily and what their magickal significance would be if used intentionally.

Spellwork essentials

- Use a notebook to test out any spells or rituals before copying the perfected version to your grimoire (see page 22).
- Take time to consider the intentions of your spell or ritual, as well as all possible outcomes – especially if involving others.
- If in doubt, do a divination session (for example, using tarot cards, or a pendulum) to assess if the spell is a good idea or not.
- Use ingredients that correspond with your intentions (see pages 178–185). Remember you cannot make carrot cake without carrots – any substitutions need to make sense.
- Ingredients can also include sigils, runes, tokens or taglocks, and so on. It is best to use ingredients local to you and your culture. Ingredients you already have on hand can also help you work out the type of spell you want to perform.
- Consider the timing of your spell – using the moon's phases is the most common method, though you can also use astrological timing, such as specific weekdays or hours. Special dates throughout the year can be powerful, and for certain spells or rituals consider the seasons too.
- Location can be a factor – some spells are best done outside, but not everyone has the access. Work with what you've got.
- Be as specific as possible with spells, as sometimes results are not as expected. The more detail, the better.
- Safety is essential, especially when working with elements, or with ingredients that could potentially cause harm – always practise safely!
- Spells may need to be revised or redone.

Spell type

Certain spell types are better suited for certain spells than others: jars and charm bags contain energies; sympathetic spells are one of the oldest forms of magick, using one thing to represent another (such as puppets, candles, paintings, and so on); and knot spells tie or release things.

Think about what each form naturally represents, and how you can use it in your spellwork. For example, planting seeds is related to harvesting and drawing things towards you, while using fire releases and cleanses.

Disposing of spells

Some parts of a spell can be cleaned, cleansed, and reused – such as jars, crystals, and other tokens. Some elements need to be placed in the bin – such as salt, which causes soil to become infertile.

Different ways of disposing of the spell can also form part of the spell. Burning any last remnants to fully release the energies of the spell, burying near your home for drawing intentions towards you, burying far away from you if you do not want that energy anywhere near you (such as banishings), or releasing biodegradable and non-toxic ingredients into rivers or oceans can be an important final step.

Always consider that you are not alone on this planet and be mindful that certain ingredients may not be good for local animals and wildlife. When unsure, placing remnants in the bin is fine.

Spell template

Here is a simple template you can use to start writing your own spells and rituals. You can also use any spell in this book as a starting point and make it your own by adjusting it for your specific purpose.

Intentions:

Tools and ingredients:

Timing:

Location:

CORRESPONDENCES

Here are several correspondences to help you in your own spellcrafting. You may not resonate with every associated correspondence and some will differ across cultures, so go with your own intuition and make logical substitutions.

Colours

These are the common colour associations, though depending on the person and the culture, they may vary.

WHITE Purification, Healing, Blessings, Protection, Substitute for any other colour

BLACK Protection, Banishing and binding, Ancestors, Spirit work, Honouring death

BROWN Home, Stability, Growth and strength, Earth

RED Passion, Power, Sex and libido, Strength, Element: fire

ORANGE Creativity, Inspiration, Good luck, Success, Positivity, Communication

YELLOW Happiness, Clarity and memory, Communication, Energy, Element: air

GREEN Healing, Fertility, Growth, Abundance, Luck, Balance, Prosperity, Element: earth

BLUE Peace and calm, Wisdom, Renewal and forgiveness, Healing and protection, Element: water

PURPLE Psychic abilities, Intuition, Divination, Higher realms

PINK Love, Friendship, Beauty, Self-love

SILVER Spirituality and intuition, Dreams, Lunar energies, Female divinity

GOLD Success, Wealth, Attraction, Male divinity

Moon phases

Days of the week

You may prefer to break down the moon phases into simple (New Moon, Waxing Moon, Full Moon, Waning Moon) or more detailed phases (Waxing Crescent, First Quarter, and so on). These are the common associations with each phase.

These are the commonly associated correspondences used mostly in European countries – work with these or with a set that feels suitable to your practice. A lot of deities and spirits have certain days associated with them, something you may want to take into consideration if you are working with any.

 NEW MOON
New beginnings, Manifestations, Cleansing and protection, Shadow work, Divination

 WAXING CRESCENT
Intentions, Attraction and motivation, Success

 FIRST QUARTER
Creativity, Growth, Action, Love

 WAXING GIBBOUS
Refine and analyse, Good health, Attraction

 FULL MOON
Charging, Cleansing, Power, Healing, A good time for all spells

 WANING GIBBOUS
Undoing, Bidding, Baneful workings, Cleansing

 THIRD QUARTER
Breaking bad habits, Banishing, Breaking curses

 WANING CRESCENT
Gratitude, Wisdom, Letting go

 MONDAY – MOON
Purity, Spirituality, Cleansing, Lunar power, Magick and divination, Healing, Female energies

 TUESDAY – MARS
Strength, Energy, Passion, Motivation, Movement, Ambition, Male energies, Banishing

 WEDNESDAY – MERCURY
Knowledge, Communication, Art and creativity, Confidence, Travel and change

 THURSDAY – JUPITER
Luck, Growth, Success and fulfilment, Oaths and treaties

 FRIDAY – VENUS AND EARTH
Fertility, Love, Sex, Romance, Prosperity, Female power, Family and friends

 SATURDAY – SATURN
Law and contracts, Changing and renewing, Protection, Freedom

 SUNDAY – SUN
Solar power, Success and victory, Empowerment, Material wealth and possessions, Health and vitality, Male power

Crystals

Crystals, while not inherently part of witchcraft, have been used for centuries in all cultures around the world, either for adornment or magickal purposes such as protection, divination, and amplifying energy. These are the most common crystal associations, but by no means is this an exhaustive list of all crystals and their common correspondences. Try meditating with a crystal to see what energies you pick up – they may differ from the regular association. Clear Quartz, the "Mother of Crystals", can substitute all other crystals as well as amplify the power of other crystals when used alongside them.

AGATE Health, Joy, Serenity

ALEXANDRITE Work, Ambition

AMAZONITE Friendship, Communication, Work, Ambition

AMBER Protection, Personal growth, Health, Love, Sex, Work, Ambition

AMETHYST Protection, Personal growth, Health, Friendship, Communication

AMETRINE Health

ANGELITE Friendship, Communication

APATITE Friendship, Communication

AQUAMARINE Health, Prosperity, Joy, Serenity, Work, Ambition

AZURITE Personal growth, Friendship, Communication

BLOODSTONE Protection, Work, Ambition

BLUE LACE AGATE Personal growth, Health, Friendship, Communication, Joy, Serenity

CALCITE Protection, Health

CARNELIAN Protection, Health, Work, Ambition

CELESTITE Health, Friendship, Communication

CHAROITE Personal growth

CHRYSOCOLLA Friendship, Communication

CHRYSOPRASE Health

CITRINE Prosperity, Health, Friendship, Communication, Joy, Serenity, Work, Ambition

CLEAR QUARTZ Protection, Prosperity, Health, Friendship, Communication

DIAMOND Protection, Prosperity, Love, Sex, Work, Ambition

FLOWER AGATE Prosperity

FLUORITE Personal growth, Friendship, Communication

GARNET Protection, Love, Sex, Work, Ambition

GREEN QUARTZ Prosperity

HEMATITE Protection

HONEY CALCITE Prosperity, Joy, Serenity

JADE Work, Ambition

JASPER Health

JET Protection

LABRADORITE Protection, Personal growth, Work, Ambition

LARIMAR Health

LEPIDOLITE Protection, Joy, Serenity

MALACHITE Protection, Prosperity, Personal growth, Work, Ambition

MOLDAVITE Personal growth

MOONSTONE Personal growth, Health, Love, Sex, Friendship, Communication

MORGANITE Love, Sex

MOSS AGATE Friendship, Communication

OBSIDIAN Protection, Personal growth, Joy, Serenity

OCEAN JASPER Joy, Serenity

ONYX Protection

OPAL Prosperity, Work, Ambition

PERIDOT Prosperity, Work, Ambition

PETRIFIED WOOD Health

PINK OPAL Love, Sex

PYRITE Prosperity, Work, Ambition

QUARTZ CRYSTAL Protection

RED JASPER Protection

RHODOCHROSITE Love, Sex, Friendship, Communication

RHODONITE Love, Sex, Joy, Serenity

ROSE QUARTZ Health, Love, Sex, Friendship, Communication, Joy, Serenity

RUBY Prosperity

SALT Protection, Health, Work, Ambition

SAPPHIRE Work, Ambition

SATIN SPAR Protection, Friendship, Communication, Joy, Serenity

SELENITE Protection, Friendship, Communication, Joy, Serenity

SMOKY QUARTZ Protection

SNOWFLAKE OBSIDIAN Protection

SODALITE Personal growth, Joy, Serenity, Health

SUNSTONE Health, Work, Ambition

TIGER'S EYE Prosperity, Personal growth, Protection, Friendship, Communication, Work, Ambition

TURQUOISE Protection, Prosperity, Friendship, Communication

UNAKITE Joy, Serenity

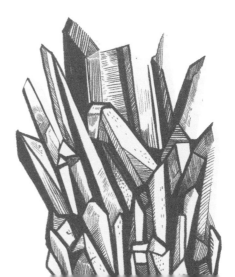

Elements and cardinal directions

These are the traditional associations, but if these don't seem to make much sense to you and where you live, consider changing them. For example, if you live in an area with lots of wind coming from the north, then change the cardinal directions so they suit you.

• A note about the southern hemisphere: some people like to flip all the associations of the directions (meaning east and west are also flipped) whereas some only swap north and south. Again, it is entirely up to you and what makes most sense to you.

ELEMENTAL MAGICK TIMING

EARTH Slowest element, growing and moving with time

AIR Moves freely, often related to thoughts, ideas

FIRE Fastest element, burning, releases energy almost instantly, not usually long-lasting

WATER Slow and steady, often related to emotion or life energy

NORTHERN HEMISPHERE

NORTH Earth

EAST Air

SOUTH Fire

WEST Water

SOUTHERN HEMISPHERE

NORTH Fire

EAST Air

SOUTH Earth

WEST Water

Herbs and plants

Herbs and plants are not only important in everyday life but have been used across cultures both for eating and spiritual matters. Please be cautious when using plants or herbs – research each one before using it, especially when ingesting it (a lot of plants are toxic) and be aware of any possible allergic reactions before using any herb or plant. Naturally, this list is not exhaustive, and you may find certain correspondences here don't align with your usual associations – always go with what feels right for you.

A

ALMOND Money, Prosperity

ALOE Peace, Healing, Success, Prosperity

ANGELICA Protection, Banishing, Healing, Psychic abilities

ANISE SEED Protection, Purification, Protected sleep

APPLE Protection, Love, Healing

ARNICA Healing

ASH Protection, Prosperity, Healing

AVOCADO Love, Beauty, Sexual desire

B

BAMBOO Protection, Banishing, Good fortune, Success

BANANA Prosperity, Fertility

BARLEY Love, Healing, Protection

BASIL Protection, Love, Prosperity, Psychic abilities

BAY Protection, Purification, Healing, Strength, Psychic abilities, Manifestation

BERGAMOT Prosperity, Good fortune, Clarity

BIRCH Protection, Banishing, Purification

BLACK PEPPER Protection, Banishing, Defensive

BLACKBERRY Protection, Prosperity, Healing

BLUEBERRIES Protection, Home protection

BUCKTHORN Protection, Banishing, Success, Contracts

C

CACTUS Protection, Defensive

CAMOMILE Protection, Peace, Sleep, Banishing, Purification, Prosperity

CARDAMOM Love, Sexual desire

CARNATION Protection, Strength, Healing

CARROTS Healing, Fertility, Sexual desire

CATNIP Love, Beauty, Happiness

CEDAR Protection, Purification, Healing, Prosperity

CELANDINE Protection, Happiness, Contracts

CHERRY Love, Divination

CHILLI PEPPER Hex-breaking, Love

CHOCOLATE Good fortune, Sexual desire, Happiness

CHRYSANTHEMUM Protection

CINNAMON Prosperity, Protection, Success, Healing

CLOVE Protection, Banishing, Love, Money, Healing

CLOVER Protection, Banishing, Love, Success

COCONUT Protection, Purification

COFFEE Protection, Banishing, Passion, Strength, Sexual desire

COMFREY Protection, Travel, Money

CORIANDER Protection, Love, Healing

CROCUS Love, Divination

CUMIN Protection, Banishing

D

DAFFODIL Love, Fertility, Good fortune

DAISIES Love, Happiness

DANDELION Healing, Divination, Success

DILL Protection, Money, Love, Sexual desire

DRAGON'S BLOOD Protection, Banishing, Love, Fertility

E

EDELWEISS Protection, Success

ELDERBERRY Protection, Banishing, Healing, Sleep, Prosperity

EUCALYPTUS Protection, Healing

F

FENNEL Protection, Purification, Healing

FERN Protection, Banishing, Prosperity, Money, Healing

FIG Divination, Love, Fertility

FRANKINCENSE Protection, Banishing, Psychic abilities

G

GARDENIA Psychic abilities, Peace, Healing, Love

GARLIC Protection, Banishing, Healing, Sexual desire

GERANIUM Protection, Healing, Fertility, Love

GINGER Healing, Money, Success, Power, Love

GINSENG Protection, Healing, Success, Love, Beauty

H

HAWTHORN Protection, Happiness, Fertility

HEATHER Protection, Good fortune

HEMP Healing, Psychic abilities, Peace

HIBISCUS Divination, Love, Sexual desire

HIGH JOHN THE CONQUEROR Money, Happiness, Love

HOLLY Protection, Good fortune

HONEYSUCKLE Protection, Psychic abilities, Money

HYACINTH Protection, Happiness, Love

I

IVY Protection, Healing, Divination

J

JASMINE Protection, Dreams, Money, Love

JUNIPER Protection, Banishing, Healing, Love

L

LADY'S MANTLE Love

LAVENDER Protection, Purification, Happiness, Healing, Sleep, Love, Peace

LEMON Protection, Banishing, Purification, Love, Friendship

LEMON VERBENA Purification, Love

LILAC Protection, Banishing

LILY Protection, Hex-breaking, Strength

LILY OF THE VALLEY Protection, Happiness, Psychic abilities

LIME Protection, Healing, Love, Good fortune

LOTUS Protection

M

MANDARIN Healing, Happiness, Good fortune

MANDRAKE Protection, Prosperity, Love, Healing, Fertility, Psychic abilities, Dreams

MAPLE Happiness, Love, Prosperity

MARIGOLD Protection, Psychic abilities, Contracts, Happiness

MARJORAM Protection, Prosperity, Happiness, Love, Healing

MINT Protection, Banishing, Travel, Prosperity, Money, Sexual desire

MISTLETOE Protection, Banishing, Good fortune, Love, Healing

MOSS Money, Good fortune

MUGWORT Protection, Psychic abilities, Dreams, Strength, Healing

MYRRH Protection, Banishing, Healing, Psychic abilities

MYRTLE Peace, Love, Money, Fertility

N

NUTMEG Prosperity, Good fortune, Healing

O

OAK Protection, Healing, Money, Good fortune, Fertility

ONION Protection, Banishing, Prosperity, Healing, Psychic abilities, Sexual desire

ORANGE Good fortune, Prosperity, Psychic abilities, Love

P

PAPAYA Protection, Love

PATCHOULI Sexual desire, Money, Fertility

PEACH Banishing, Love, Fertility, Success

PEONY Protection, Banishing

PEPPERMINT Purification, Sleep, Psychic abilities, Healing, Love, Prosperity

POMEGRANATE Psychic abilities, Success, Money, Fertility

POPPY Money, Success, Love, Sleep, Fertility

POTATO Protection, Prosperity

PRIMROSE Protection, Love

PUMPKIN Prosperity, Manifesting

R

RASPBERRY Protection, Love

ROSE Protection, Psychic abilities, Healing, Good fortune, Love, Sexual desire

ROSEMARY Protection, Banishing, Purification, Healing, Psychic abilities, Sleep, Love, Sexual desire

ROWAN Protection, Success, Healing, Psychic abilities

RUE Banishing, Hex-breaking, Healing, Psychic abilities, Love

S

SAFFRON Healing, Strength, Happiness, Love, Sexual desire, Psychic abilities

SAGE Protection, Purification, Success, Wisdom

SANDALWOOD Protection, Banishing, Success, Healing, Psychic abilities

SOLOMON'S SEAL Protection, Banishing, Good fortune

ST. JOHN'S WORT Protection, Strength, Happiness, Healing

STAR ANISE Protection, Psychic abilities, Good fortune

STRAWBERRY Love, Good fortune

SUGAR (CANE) Love, Sexual desire

SUNFLOWER Wisdom, Healing, Success, Fertility, Happiness

T

THISTLE Protection, Banishing, Hex-breaking, Healing, Strength

THORNS Protection, Defensive

THYME Purification, Sleep, Psychic abilities, Healing, Love, Courage

TURMERIC Purification, Healing

V

VALERIAN Protection, Purification, Sleep, Love

VANILLA Psychic abilities, Love, Sexual desire, Happiness

VERVAIN Protection, Purification, Peace, Prosperity, Healing, Sleep, Love

VIOLET Protection, Success, Peace, Healing, Sexual desire, Love, Good fortune

W

WALNUT Protection, Psychic abilities, Success, Healing

WILLOW Protection, Healing, Love

WITCH HAZEL Protection, Banishing, Healing

WORMWOOD Protection, Psychic abilities, Love

INDEX

A

All Hallows Eve 153
altar
  ancestor altar 124
  setting up 20–23
amber 88
amulets/talismans
  abracadabra healing amulet spell 85
  charming talisman spell 164
  emotional healing talisman 97
  enchanted amber amulet spell 88
  piece of your pet talisman 123
  talisman enchantment 31
  wishbone talisman 60
animal family 122–123
  pet bed spell 123
  piece of your pet talisman 123
anti-anxiety spell jar 148
athame 23
atheist witches 13
autumn equinox 153

B

banishing harm 38–41
  all-round protection 40–41
  hex-removing bath 40
  return to sender 39
  see also illness banishment bathing
broken heart bath ritual 112
career success shower pouch 159
hex-removing bath 40
lavender bath 137

lovers bath ritual 102
manifestation bath ritual 158
self-love bath spell 73
Waning Moon bathing ritual 89
bayleaf spell for happiness 140
bed spray recipe 85
bells 27
besom 23
beyond the veil 124–125
  All Hallows Eve 153
  connecting to ancestors ritual 124
  farewell ritual 125
black salt 32
"black and white magick" 19
blues-banishing ritual 149
bowls
  prosperity bowl 49
  self-love bowl 71
  sweet boss bowl 167
broken heart bath ritual 112

C

candles 11, 20
  13-day candle spell 163
  break-up cord-cutting spell 114–115
  colour correspondences 20, 178
  distance healing candle 95
  empowerment candle 67
  healing candle ritual 94
  I am worthy candle ritual 173
  lover come to me candle 111
  lucky horseshoe candle spell 63
  money candle spell 52

resolving a fight candle spell 128
simple wishing candle 58
cardinal directions 182
career success
  charming talisman spell 164
  fast employment charm bag 165
  finding a new job spell 166
  see also success, summoning
carving tools 23
casting a circle 23, 26–27
cauldron 22
chalice 23
chaos magick 11, 13
charm bags
  abundance charm bag 57
  better sex pillow pouch 102
  fast employment charm bag 165
  mental clarity charm bag 151
  peaceful sleep charm bag 147
  psychic charm bag 68
cleansing 27
clothing
  charmed clothing 161
  enchanted shoes 161
coins: charming a coin spell 56
colds, banishing 81
colour associations 178
communication, enhanced 126–131
  better communication 129
  contact me spell 129
  mirror spell for self-reflection 131
  patience crystal meditation 126
  resolving a fight candle spell 128
  seeing the truth 126

contact me spell 129
contentment, cultivating 138–143
  bayleaf spell for happiness 140
  happiness jar spell 141
  happiness manifestation 139
  happiness oil 140
  happy knot bracelet 142
correspondences 178–185
crystals 22
  abundance crystal grid 48
  calling a new friend crystal grid 132
  correspondences 180–181
  crystal cleansing 27
  dream recorder crystal enchantment 146
  good vibes crystal grid 135
  patience crystal meditation 126
curses and hexes 19
  hex-removing bath 40
  return to sender 39
  witch bottle spell 37

D

days of the week: correspondences 179
deities/gods 13
drawing love to you 108–111
  are they right for me? divination 110
  dream partner spell 109
  enchanted necklace 110
  lovely sigil 111
  lover come to me candle 111
dreamworld 144–147
  create your own dream 146
  dream recorder crystal enchantment 146
  flying ointment 144
  peaceful sleep charm bag 147
  remembering your dreams spell 145

E

elements 17, 182
emotional wellbeing 96–97, 148–151
  anti-anxiety spell jar 148
  blues-banishing ritual 149

emotional healing talisman 97
  growing roots healing ritual 96
  mental clarity charm bag 151
endings and break-ups 112–115
  break-up cord-cutting spell 114–115
  broken heart bath ritual 112
  goodbye sock spell 113
  letting go of the ex ritual 114
energy cleansing 27
energy cleansing spray 34

F

farewell ritual 125
fire
  bring in the light fire 61
  fire scrying ritual 154
floor wash
  happy home 117
  prosperity 48
flying ointment 144
food and drink
  bread baking ritual 152
  enchanted hot chocolate 136
  good health soup 92
  harmony honey cakes 117
  peaceful hearth pie 120
  pumpkin soup 153
  rekindling the spark muffins 99
  silent supper 153
  tea see tea
forgiving yourself ritual 76
friends, making 132–133
  calling a new friend crystal grid 132
  friends bracelet knot magic 133
friendship and family magick 116–133
Full Moon cleansing 27
Full Moon ritual 44

G

garden and plants
  absorbing potato spell 81
  family garden ritual 118

herb and plant correspondences 182–185
  money tree ritual 49
  protection plant spell 35
garter charm 103
glamour 106–107
  clear skin glamour spell 88
  glamour box ritual 70
  lipstick enchantment 106
  love potion 107
gratitude ritual 79
grimoire 17, 22, 175
grounding and centring yourself 27
growing roots healing ritual 96

H

hag stone blessing 35
"harm none" 12
health spell jar 86
health and wellbeing magick 80–97
  see also emotional wellbeing;
  wellness and healing
home: finding a new home
  manifestation ritual 168
home, harmonious 117–121
  family garden ritual 118
  happy home floor wash 117
  harmony honey cakes 117
  lovely living room jar spell 121
  peaceful hearth pie 120
home, protection for the 32–37
  black salt 32
  energy cleansing spray 34
  hag stone blessing 35
  protected home ritual 36
  protection plant spell 35
  sleep protection pouch 34
  witch bottle spell 37

I

illness banishment 81–83
  absorbing potato spell 81
  release illness knot magic 82

tea to banish colds 81
incense 20
 smoke cleansing 27
intuition 68

J

joy and serenity magick 135–155

K

knot magick 11, 22
 friends bracelet knot magic 133
 happy knot bracelet 142
 reaching your goals knot spell
  171
 release illness knot magic 82
 tying the knot love spell 104

L

lipstick enchantment 106
love potion 107
love and sex magick 15, 98–115
lucky horseshoe candle spell 63

M

magic/magick 10
May Day – maypole ritual 155
mental clarity charm bag 151
microcosm and macrocosm theory
 17
mirror spell for self-reflection 131
money, attracting 47–53
 abundance charm bag 57
 abundance crystal grid 48
 charming a coin spell 56
 enchanted wallet spell 54
 money candle spell 52
 money sigil spell 56
 money tree daily ritual 49
 prosperity bowl ritual 49
 prosperity floor wash 48
 prosperity jar 51

prosperity oil 47
 prosperity spell 57
 prosperity tea 47
 prosperity witch ladder 53
moon phases 15, 179
morning ritual 78
mortar and pestle 23

N

necklace, enchanted 110

O

ocean wishing spell 58
oils
 balance oil 135
 empowerment oil 65
 happiness oil 140
 health oil 84
 prosperity oil 47
 protection oil 30
 romantic love oil 99

P

patience crystal meditation 126
pentagram 23
personal growth magick 64–79
prosperity magick 46–63
prosperity spell 57
protection magick 28–45

R

releasing the past 77
romance 99–105
 better sex pillow pouch 102
 blessed garter charm 103
 divine connection spell 101
 lovers bath ritual 102
 rekindling the spark muffins
  99
 romantic love oil 99
 tying the knot love spell 104

"rule of three" 12
runes 21, 23

S

seasonal celebrations 152–155
 All Hallows Eve 153
 autumn equinox 153
 first harvest 152
 first spring 154
 May Day 155
 spring equinox 155
 summer solstice 152
 winter solstice 154
self-dedication ritual 66
self-improvement 170–173
 I am worthy candle ritual 173
 reaching your goals knot spell 171
 sweeping away doubt ritual 170
self-love and beauty 70–73
 glamour box ritual 70
 more confidence sigil 70
 self-love bath spell 73
 self-love bowl ritual 71
self-realization and empowerment
 65–67
 empowerment candle 67
 empowerment oil 65
 personal growth sigil 65
 psychic charm bag 68
 psychic enhancement tea 68
 self-dedication ritual 66
self-reflection 74–77
 accepting your shadows ritual 75
 forgiving yourself ritual 76
 mirror spell for self-reflection 131
 releasing the past 77
 shadow work ritual 74
serenity, summoning 135–137
 balance oil 135
 enchanted hot chocolate 136
 good vibes crystal grid 135
 lavender bath ritual 137
 morning tea spell 136
shadow self

accepting your shadows ritual 75
shadow work ritual 74
shielding for empaths ritual 29
sigils 22, 23
   good health sigil 86
   lovely sigil 111
   money sigil spell 56
   more confidence sigil 70
   personal growth sigil 65
sleep
   peaceful sleep charm bag 147
   sleep protection pouch 34
   see also dreamworld
smoke cleansing 27
sound cleansing 27
spell book see grimoire
spell jars 11, 23
   anti-anxiety spell jar 148
   happiness jar spell 141
   health spell jar 86
   lovely living room jar spell 121
   prosperity jar 51
   protection jar 42
   witch bottle spell 37
spells
   adapting and personalizing 11, 13,
      178–183
   disposing of 176
   how spells work 16–17
   knowing what you want from 14, 15
   timing 15, 175
   writing your own spells 174–177
spirit offering ritual 43
spring equinox – ostara eggs spell
   155
staff 23
success, summoning 157–169
   13-day candle spell 163
   career success shower pouch
      159
   charmed clothing spell 161
   enchanted shoes sigil 161
   manifestation bath ritual 158
   ringing in customers doorbell spell 159
   success powder 157

sun water ritual 157
sweet boss bowl spell 167
Waxing Moon ritual 162
see also career success
summer solstice – flower crown
   ritual 152
sun water ritual 157

T

talismans see amulets/ talismans
tarot cards 23, 175
tea
   intentional coffee or tea daily ritual 79
   morning tea spell 136
   prosperity tea 47
   psychic enhancement tea 68
   tea to banish colds 81
travel protection pouch 30
truth, seeing the 126

W

wallet: enchanted wallet spell 54
wand/staff 23
Waning Moon bathing ritual 89
Waxing Moon ritual 162
wellness and healing 84–95
   abracadabra healing amulet spell 85
   clear skin glamour spell 88
   distance healing candle 95
   enchanted Amber amulet spell 88
   enchanted hair and toothbrush ritual
      91
   good health bed spray recipe 85
   good health sigil 86
   good health soup 92
   healing candle ritual 94
   healing salve recipe 93
   health oil 84
   health spell jar 86
   Waning Moon bathing ritual 89
Wicca 12
winter solstice – blessed yule log
   ritual 154

wishbone talisman 60
witch bottle spell 37
witch ladder 53
witchcraft
   ethical 18–19
   karmic concepts 12
   open and closed practices 18–19
   spells see spells
   understanding the consequences of 19
work and ambition magick 156–173

Sources

PAGES 10–11: Lipscomb, Suzannah, *A History of Magic, Witchcraft and the Occult,* DK, 2020.

PAGES 12–13: Mooney, Thorn, *Traditional Wicca: A Seeker's Guide,* Llewellyn Worldwide, 2018.

PAGES 16–17: Agrippa, Henry Cornelius, *Three Books of Occult Philosophy,* Llewellyn Worldwide, 2005.

Adler, Margot, *Drawing Down the Moon,* Penguin, 1979.

Farrar, Janet and Stewart, *Spells and How They Work,* Open Road Integrated Media, 2012.

PAGES 18–19: Valiente, Doreen, *The Charge of the Goddess: The Poetry of Doreen Valiente,* Doreen Valiente Foundation, 2014.

PAGE 26: DuQuette, Lon Milo, Shoemaker, David, Skinner, Stephen, *Llewellyn's Complete Book of Ceremonial Magick: A Comprehensive Guide to the Western Mystery Tradition*, Llewellyn Worldwide, 2020.

PAGES 26–27 AND PAGE 29: Auryn, Mat, *Psychic Witch: A Metaphysical Guide to Meditation, Magick & Manifestation,* Llewellyn Worldwide, 2020.

PAGES 29–45: Miller, Jason, *Protection & Reversal Magick: A Witch's Defense Manual,* New Page Books, 2006.

PAGES 144–147: Hatsis, Thomas, *The Witches' Ointment: The Secret History of Psychedelic Magic,* Inner Traditions/Bear & Company, 2015.

PAGE 155: Hutton, Ronald, *The Witch: A History of Fear, from Ancient Times to the Present,* Yale University Press, 2017.

PAGES 178–183 and throughout: Kynes, Sandra, *Llewellyn's Complete Book of Essential Oils: How to Blend, Diffuse, Create Remedies, and Use in Everyday Life,* Llewellyn Worldwide, 2019.

Kynes, Sandra, *Llewellyn's Complete Book of Correspondences: A Comprehensive & Cross-Referenced Resource for Pagans & Wiccans,* Llewellyn Worldwide, 2013.

Pradas, Lidia, *The Complete Grimoire: Magickal Practices and Spells for Awakening Your Inner Witch,* Fair Winds Press, 2020.

Valiente, Doreen, *An ABC of Witchcraft Past and Present,* Robert Hale Non-Fiction, 2018.

PAGES 179–180: Hall, Judy, *The Crystal Bible,* Godsfield Press, 2003.

PAGES 181–183: Cunningham, Scott, *Cunningham's Encyclopedia of Magical Herbs,* Llewellyn Worldwide, 2012.

Disclaimer

About the Author

Ella Harrison has been a practising witch for over 10 years, and she aspires to inspire and educate people about witchcraft and pagan practices. Ella is best known for her YouTube channel where she creates beginner-friendly videos on Wicca and witchcraft. Ella was born in New Zealand and raised in a German family who practise various aspects of witchcraft. She holds a degree in social and cultural anthropology and creates content on YouTube, Instagram, and TikTok. Ella and her husband, Karlis, co-own a small crystal business called Silverfern Crystals (ekstones.com).

Acknowledgments

Author's Acknowledgments

Thank you dear reader, I do not take it lightly that you picked up my book and dedicated your time to reading it. Without you, and all the support I have received in person as well as online, I would truly not have had the opportunity to write this book, and I am forever grateful for you.

Thank you my love and husband, Karlis, for always believing in me, supporting me, and of course keeping me hydrated and caffeinated as well as bringing me my phone charger during the writing process. I cannot logically say thank you to my two fluffy boys Chip and Bennie as they refuse to speak, but their cuddles and licks were much appreciated throughout the writing of this book (and beyond). A special thank you to Hannah and Autumn for being further emotional support, as well as general witch inspiration.

Of course, none of this book could be what it is without my incredible editor Emma – thank you for always answering any questions I had and helping me in the writing of this book. I would not have known where to start without your guidance.

Thank you to the entire DK team, this whole process was incredible and I am so grateful for this experience, what an opportunity!

And last, but most definitely not least, thank you to my family – to my Mama and Oma for introducing me to tarot, crystals, spirits, and magick, and raising me to be the witch I am today, and to Papa for supporting and sponsoring it and being the calm and supportive person throughout it all. To my dad and stepmum, who likely are unaware of how important that first spell and dream book was that I fished out of a "below $5" book bin when I was a child, and who were always supportive of my witchy interests. To Opa, my very first editor when I tried writing as a teenager, for supporting my creative endeavours. Who would have thought I would ever actually realize that childhood dream? And naturally this acknowledgment section could not be written without my (second) biggest fan, Kind – sorry, Julia! (I say second as Karlis will likely be upset if I do not list him as first).

Publisher's Acknowledgments

DK would like to thank Aleksandra Czudżak for her tireless work and beautiful illustrations, John Friend for proofreading, and Marie Lorimer for the index.

Senior Project Editor	Emma Hill
Senior Art Editors	Tom Forge and Emma Forge
Senior Editor	Dawn Titmus
Project Designer	Louise Brigenshaw
Project Editor	Izzy Holton
Jacket Designer	Amy Cox
Jacket Coordinator	Jasmin Lennie
Senior Production Editor	Tony Phipps
Senior Producer	Luca Bazzoli
Editorial Manager	Ruth O'Rourke
Design Manager	Marianne Markham
Art Director	Maxine Pedliham
Publishing Director	Katie Cowan
Illustrator	Aleksandra Czudżak

First published in Great Britain in 2022 by
Dorling Kindersley Limited
DK, One Embassy Gardens, 8 Viaduct Gardens,
London, SW11 7BW

The authorized representative in the EEA is
Dorling Kindersley Verlag GmbH.
Arnulfstr. 124, 80636 Munich, Germany

A CIP catalogue record for this book
is available from the British Library.
ISBN: 978-0-2415-4865-3

Printed and bound in Slovakia

www.dk.com

This book was made with Forest
Stewardship Council™ certified
paper – one small step in DK's
commitment to a sustainable future.
**For more information go to
www.dk.com/our-green-pledge**